How to Use

MICROSOFT
FRONTPAGE 97
FOR WINDOWS

How to Use

MICROSOFT FRONTPAGE 97 FOR WINDOWS

CELINE LATULIPE
WITH **DAVID KARLINS** AND
ELAINE MADISON

Ziff-Davis Press
An imprint of Macmillan Computer Publishing USA
Emeryville, California

Publisher	Stacy Hiquet
Acquisitions Editors	Suzanna Anthony and Lucresia Ashford
Editor	Margo Hill
Technical Reviewer	David Karlins
Production Editor	Ami Knox
Proofreader	Kayla Sussell
Cover Illustration and Design	Megan Gandt
Book Design	Dennis Gallagher/Visual Strategies, San Francisco
Page Layout	Janet Piercy
Indexer	Richard Genova

Ziff-Davis Press, ZD Press, and the Ziff-Davis Press logo are trademarks or registered trademarks of, and are licensed to Macmillan Computer Publishing USA by Ziff-Davis Publishing Company, New York, New York.

Ziff-Davis Press imprint books are produced on a Macintosh computer system with the following applications: FrameMaker®, Microsoft® Word, QuarkXPress®, Adobe Illustrator®, Adobe Photoshop®, Adobe Streamline™, MacLink® *Plus*, Aldus® FreeHand™, Collage Plus™.

Ziff-Davis Press, an imprint of
Macmillan Computer Publishing USA
5903 Christie Avenue
Emeryville, CA 94608

ISBN 1-56276-462-4

Manufactured in the United States of America
10 9 8 7 6 5 4 3 2

DEDICATION

To Rob, who interrupted my work on this book to propose. Thanks for asking!

TABLE OF CONTENTS

ACKNOWLEDGMENTS

I'd like to thank everyone at Ziff-Davis Press, especially Suzanne Anthony, Margo Hill, and Lucresia Ashford. My tech editor, Dave Karlins, also deserves thanks. Without these people, this book would not exist. I'd like to thank Neil Randall, because without him, my writing career wouldn't ever have begun. I'd like to thank my friends at NCR who supported me and put up with my yawning whenever I'd been up late the previous evening to work on this book. I'd like to thank all my close friends for being out of the country at a convenient time — with them around I never would have gotten anything done! Most of all though, I'd like to thank Rob. He was constantly neglected while I worked on this book, yet remained supportive throughout.

INTRODUCTION

 The World Wide Web and the Internet started out as a forum for research and education. It wasn't originally meant to support the public. But the public jumped in anyhow, and now the Internet is this wonderful international communications network that brings people from all over the world together. At first, people who weren't computer scientists were limited to communicating with e-mail and through the newsgroups. They could surf the Web, but the average person couldn't distribute information over the Web because it required hardware access and software know-how. Both of these barriers have crumbled considerably over the past two years. Now, when people get an Internet account, they can usually acquire or rent server space at the same time without a lot of extra hassle or cost. And, it is no longer necessary to learn how to use HTML in order to create a Web page or an entire Web site. Microsoft FrontPage is one of a number of software programs that allows you to create Web pages without typing a single HTML tag. It is one of the very first programs that really makes Web page creation just as easy as using a word processing program to write a letter. And, because Microsoft FrontPage contains the same interface as the other programs in Microsoft Office, many people will be able to learn FrontPage in no time at all!

There may be some computer specialists who resent the fact that Microsoft is once again bringing computing to the average person, instead of leaving it in the hands of the experts. I am not one of those computer specialists. I think that the Web is a tool that will open up many markets and fields to the public. No longer is the public limited to watching the commercials and the television shows that people with money are dishing out. Now the public can get on the Internet and dish it right back. The Internet gives anyone who is starting out in any profession or field or hobby access to information and people who would otherwise be out of reach. A new musician can make her music available to a global audience, a student in Australia can make his thesis and research information available to academics all over the globe, and an entrepreneur in Iceland can advertise and sell his products to a global audience. All of these things can be achieved by anyone who has access to the Internet and a willingness to learn a little bit. Microsoft FrontPage makes doing all of these things really easy, and in this book I hope to show you how!

Celine Latulipe
clatulip@cgl.uwaterloo.ca
clatulip@watarts.uwaterloo.c

CHAPTER 1

Your Web Site and the World

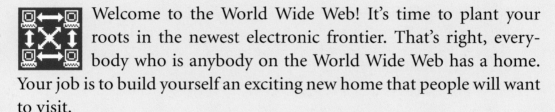 Welcome to the World Wide Web! It's time to plant your roots in the newest electronic frontier. That's right, everybody who is anybody on the World Wide Web has a home. Your job is to build yourself an exciting new home that people will want to visit.

Since you've purchased Microsoft FrontPage 97, it's probably safe to assume that you know enough about the World Wide Web to want to get on right away and create a Web site for yourself. This book assumes that you have at least a 486 computer running Windows, and that you have an Internet account—these are the minimum requirements to run Microsoft FrontPage 97. If you don't have an Internet account yet, don't worry. You'll learn how to get set up with an Internet account later in this chapter.

The World Wide Web can get pretty complicated when you start investigating the nitty-gritty details of how it works. Fortunately, there's FrontPage 97, which allows you to build a Web site without learning about those nitty-gritty details. However, before you set out to create the site of the century, you should really set out and explore the Web. That way you'll have an idea of what makes a good Web site (and what makes a truly awful one).

How to Plug into the World Wide Web

If you don't have access to the World Wide Web yet, either through your office, school, or a commercial Internet service provider, your first assignment is to get access—at the minimum, you'll need to get yourself a modem and a dial-up PPP account. Look in the yellow pages under Internet Service Providers to find out about Internet services offered in your area. And you'll need to get yourself some space on one of the Internet Service Provider's servers, so that you have a property on which to build your new Web home. If you don't get space on your Service Provider's server, you will have to keep your Web site on your local hard disk. This means leaving your computer on and your dial-up account active 24 hours a day, seven days a week, for people to access your Web site. For most people, this is not a viable option.

On these two pages, we'll show you how to get the things you need to get on the Web. If you already have an Internet account and server space, skip this section and go on to the next; you're ready to start building a Web.

TIP SHEET

▶ **What if I can't get any server space? Can I still use FrontPage 97?** Yes, you sure can! You can use the Personal Web Server to create Web pages on your own computer. However, people on the Internet won't be able to see your pages until you get yourself some server space and upload your pages.

▶ **How much server space do you need?** If you're just creating a home page for yourself, 10 megabytes will probably suffice. If you're creating business Web pages, you may need more.

▶ For those who do want information about the Web and how it works, you can find out where to look for it in the Appendix.

▶ **1** Make sure your computer is Internet-ready. You need a fast modem—28,800 BPS is the minimum. You should also be running Windows 95 or Windows NT and have FrontPage 97 installed.

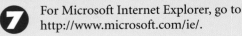

7 For Microsoft Internet Explorer, go to http://www.microsoft.com/ie/.

2 Look in your phone book or ask your friends to recommend an Internet Service Provider. Most service providers have good procedures for helping new users get online, and they usually provide some software, too.

3 Ask the service provider about getting some space on their servers for your Web site. Many providers offer some Web space as a part of their Internet packages.

4 Find out from the system administrator where your server space is located. You need to know the host name, the directory, and the login procedure. You should be given a user name and password, which may be the same ones you use when you dial in to your service provider.

5 When you get online, you'll probably be using either Netscape Navigator 3.0 or Microsoft Internet Explorer 3.0 as your Web browser. To ensure that you have the latest version of your browser, and all the newest plug-ins and add-ons available, you can visit the Navigator or Internet Explorer Web site where you can download upgrades and new add-ons.

6 For Netscape Navigator, go to http://home.netscape.com/comprod/products/navigator/index.html.

How to Use FrontPage 97 to Create Your Web Site

With FrontPage 97 installed, you're ready to start making your own Web site, an essential first step before creating any Web pages. Here we'll show you how to use FrontPage 97 to prepare your server space to hold Web pages, creating a site under a name you choose. When you create pages later on, FrontPage 97 will automatically put them in your Web site, and give them the correct URLs (Universal Resource Locators). Note: Before you start this activity, you need to make sure you know the server name and the password information to access your Web space.

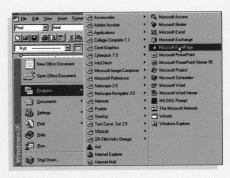

▶ ❶ Press the Windows Start button, then click on Microsoft FrontPage.

❻ You've created your first Web site! In the FrontPage 97 Explorer window you can toggle between Hyperlink View and Folder View. There are also a number of tool buttons and menus at the top of the screen.

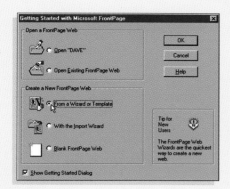

2 Select From a Template or Wizard in the Create a New FrontPage Web area and then click on the OK button in the Getting Started With Microsoft FrontPage dialog box.

3 The New FrontPage Web dialog box allows you to create a new Web from various Web site templates already built into FrontPage 97. Highlight Normal Web and click OK.

4 The Normal Web Template dialog box will appear. At this point you need to enter the name of the server where you have been allotted space, or enter default to create a web site on your own computer. Enter a name for your Web site (no spaces allowed). Click on OK.

5 FrontPage will prompt you for your Name and Password. Enter them and OK the Name and Password Required dialog box.

How to Learn More About the World Wide Web

HTML is the language used to create Web pages. It's actually a very simple computer language, but seems complex if you're not really computer literate. There is a whole lot to know about the World Wide Web, including HTML. Although you don't need to know much in order to create Web pages with Microsoft FrontPage 97, learning about the Web definitely can't hurt you. If you are interested, this page gives you a bit of information, but also points you to sources where you can learn a lot more.

▶ ❶ The computers on the Internet communicate with one another using the Internet Protocol, known as TCP/IP. The Web pages that are sent back and forth over the network using this protocol are written in a language called HTML. HTML stands for HyperText Markup Language. A server sends out an HTML document in response to a request from your Web browser. Because the browser understands HTML, it takes the HTML document and translates it into the graphical pages you see in your browser window.

❺ To learn more about how the Internet and the World Wide Web work, check out some of the following Web sites:

▶ World Wide Web FAQ: http://www.boutell.com/faq/.

▶ A Beginner's Guide to HTML: http://www.ncsa.uiuc.edu/General/Internet/ WWW/HTMLPrimer.html.

▶ A Guide to HTML Commands: http://www.woodhill.co.uk/html/html.htm.

▶ ILC Glossary of Internet Terms: http://www.matisse.net/files/glossary.html.

TIP SHEET

▶ **Because the World Wide Web is the fastest growing Internet application, the terms Internet and World Wide Web are often used synonymously. This is incorrect. The Internet actually consists of the World Wide Web, e-mail, File Transfer Protocol (ftp), and a number of other applications.**

▶ **The HTML Reference appendix at the end of this book is a good source for answers to quick questions. For a complete HTML guide, see *How to Use HTML3* from Ziff-Davis Press.**

2 In Web documents, HTML tags are used to identify how different parts of the document should be displayed on the browser screen. For example, if you want a certain word, such as "Welcome," to appear in bold on the browser screen, the HTML tags for beginning bold (<B>) and ending bold (</B>) would have to be placed around the word, like this: <B>Welcome</B>. With Microsoft FrontPage 97, you don't need to learn what the tags are in order to create a Web page.

3 Web pages are useful and interesting because of their hyperlinks—highlighted text or graphics which you can click on to move around the World Wide Web. Clicking on a hyperlink takes you either to another location in the same Web page, another page at the same Web site, or to another site altogether. This point-and-click navigation is the heart of the World Wide Web.

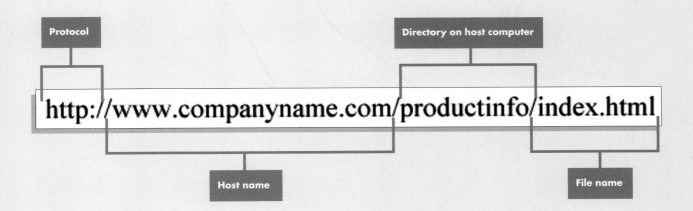

4 Universal resource locators, more commonly known as URLs, are used to create hyperlinks on World Wide Web pages. URLs have a specific layout: protocol://hostname/directory/filename. Protocol determines what type of Internet resource is being linked. A Web page would have the "http" protocol, while a program download link might have the "ftp" protocol.

CHAPTER 2

Getting Started with FrontPage 97

 Microsoft FrontPage 97 is a very comprehensive program that allows you to do a lot of different things. When you work on a Web site in FrontPage 97, you will usually have both the FrontPage Explorer and the FrontPage Editor running. You may use the Personal Server that comes with FrontPage to test your Web site. The Server Administrator allows you to configure the Server. And the TCP/IP Test program helps you find the host name and IP address that corresponds to your machine.

This chapter introduces you to each of these FrontPage 97 programs, and shows you what kind of functionality they provide. By the end of this chapter you'll be very familiar with FrontPage and you'll already have a Web site started.

How to Use the FrontPage TCP/IP Test to Determine Your Host Name

The FrontPage TCP/IP test checks to see if you are connected to the Internet, and if so, how you are connected to the Internet. In the last chapter, you tried to connect to your server so that you could set up a directory for your Web page. If you had trouble when it came to naming your host, the instructions on this page will be useful. There is one catch. If the Web space that you are using to set up your Web site doesn't happen to coincide with the server you connect to for Internet access, then the host name returned by the TCP/IP test won't be of any use to you. For instance, if you connect to the Internet through your office or school and the Web space you have is on some other server, then you'll have to get the host name from the system administrator of that server.

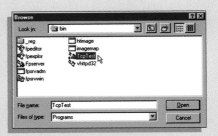

► **❶** Locate the Microsoft FrontPage folder in your Windows Run menu by clicking on the Browse button and navigating to the folder with FrontPage 97. Run the FrontPage TCPTest.

TIP SHEET

► **If you are having trouble using a remote server and you want to build a Web on your local machine, the information available in the Results Explanation window is helpful. The explanation tells you about adjustments needed in order to use the localhost server.**

► **If you are not connected when you press the Start Test button in the FrontPage TCP/IP Test dialog box, Windows 95 will bring up a Connect To dialog box, allowing you to connect to your Internet server.**

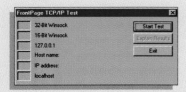

 When it is first opened, the FrontPage TCP/IP Test window has a number of empty boxes with descriptions. It also has three buttons: Start Test, Explain Results, and Exit. The Explain Results button will be dimmed when the window is first opened.

 You won't be able to do anything with this window until you hit the Start Test button. But make sure you are online before you do this!

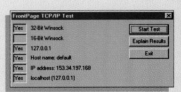

 After FrontPage has completed its TCP/IP test, it will return a "Yes" result in the boxes on the left and the Explain Results button will be active. You will also notice that the host to which you are connected is listed beside the fourth box down and that the IP address is listed beside the fifth box down. The host name that the TCP/IP test returns to you is the host name of the computer you connect to when you dial in.

 If you hit the Explain Results button in the FrontPage TCP/IP Test window, you should see a Results Explanation window. This window will tell you the host name which you can use when you want to create a new Web page. It's a good idea to scroll through this window and read all the information.

How to Use the FrontPage Explorer to Organize Your Web Site

The FrontPage Explorer has a number of options and capabilities. However, at this point, you have created a Web site that has only one Web page. Therefore, many of the options of FrontPage Explorer are not of use to you yet. On this page you'll learn how to open your pre-existing Web and a little bit about the FrontPage Explorer options you have available to you.

▶ **1** Open FrontPage. From the file menu, select Open FrontPage Web.

▶ **You can open a pre-existing Web from the frequent file list at the bottom of the File menu. This list contains the last four Webs that were open in FrontPage Explorer.**

▶ **You can toggle between Folder and Hyperlink view by selecting either option from the View menu of FrontPage Explorer.**

▶ **When you open FrontPage Explorer, FrontPage Personal Server automatically opens. (You may have noticed this from your Windows Taskbar at the bottom of your screen.) Don't worry about this for now, just leave this program running. It allows you to serve up Web pages locally.**

6 You should see FrontPage Explorer with a Folder view instead of a Hyperlink view. There are files and folders listed in the Folder view.

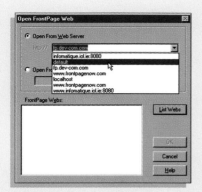

2 In the Open FrontPage Web dialog box, you should see a pull-down menu labeled Web Server. Click on the down arrow button to see the server choices. Select the server you are using for your Web site (if you are using your local computer as your server, select default or localhost). Hit the List Webs button.

3 Under the Webs label, a list of all the FrontPage Webs on the server should appear. If you are just starting to create Web sites, there will probably only be one listed, and that's the Web you created in Chapter 1. Select this Web site and click the OK button.

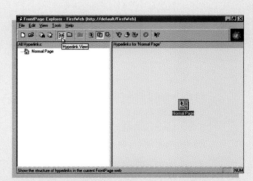

4 In the FrontPage Explorer window, you should see your Web listed in the top menu bar. You should also see the house icon with Normal Page listed beside it in the Folder view. In the Hyperlink view, you should see a single page icon.

5 There is another way to view your Web in FrontPage Explorer. If you look closely at the toolbar, you should see two buttons beside each other. One shows pages linked to a central page, and the other looks like a listing. The Hyperlink tool should be already selected. These tools allow you to toggle between Hyperlink and Folder view. Click on the Folder view button.

How to Use the FrontPage Editor to Create Web Pages

This is probably the part you've been waiting for—a chance to create a Web page, without learning any HTML. If you've used Microsoft products before, especially Microsoft Word, you will find creating Web pages with FrontPage Editor really easy. The interface of FrontPage Editor is very similar to the interface of Microsoft Word.

FrontPage Editor and FrontPage Explorer are meant to be used together. In FrontPage Explorer there is a FrontPage Editor button on the toolbar, and in FrontPage Editor there is a FrontPage Explorer button on the toolbar. These allow you to switch back and forth between the two applications easily.

TIP SHEET

▶ **You can switch from FrontPage Explorer to FrontPage Editor simply by double-clicking on a page icon in the Hyperlink view of FrontPage Explorer. FrontPage Editor will be displayed with that page open for editing.**

▶ **If you want to edit a Web page that is not part of the Web that is open in FrontPage Explorer, choose Open File from the FrontPage Editor file menu and browse through your directories to find it.**

▶ **If you want to open a Web page from somewhere on the Internet in order to edit it, choose Open Location from the FrontPage Editor file menu and type in the URL of the Web page you want to edit.**

▶ **If you open a Web page from FrontPage Editor or you create a new Web page in FrontPage Editor, you must make sure that you have your Web Site opened in FrontPage Explorer when it comes time to save your Web page. This will ensure that it is saved as part of your Web Site.**

1 In FrontPage Explorer, find the toolbar button for FrontPage Editor. It's an icon of a scroll with a feather pen. Click on this icon to open FrontPage Editor.

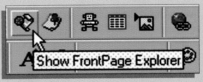

8 If you now want to go back to FrontPage Explorer to see the name change in your Web, click on the FrontPage Explorer icon on the toolbar. It's an icon of a scroll with a dart.

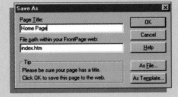

7 From the FrontPage Editor file menu, select Save As to save your Web page. The Save As dialog box will appear. You can rename this page to a name of your choice. Click OK to save.

2 The FrontPage Editor window will be displayed, but the document area will be empty and most of the toolbar buttons will be dimmed.

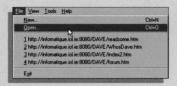

3 From the file menu, select Open.

4 Click on the Current FrontPage Web tab in the Open File dialog box. The Current FrontPage Web tab will be displayed. This window shows the Web pages available from the Web which is open in FrontPage Explorer. Select index.htm, and click on OK.

5 The Home Page will be opened in FrontPage Editor, and because this page is empty, the Editor window will still look empty. However, many of the toolbar buttons are now active. You're ready to start creating your Web home page.

6 Enter some text into the FrontPage Editor window. You've created a Web page of your own!

How to Use the FrontPage Personal Web Server to Test Your Web Site

I f you've been creating a Web site on your local machine, rather than creating it on a remote server, you can use the FrontPage Personal Web Server to test your Web site. Of course, you can always open a local file in Internet Explorer or in Netscape, but that doesn't allow you to test the parts of your Web pages that are dependent on server functionality.

At this point, you haven't created any forms, guest books, or imagemaps that depend on the server to process information and give you feedback. You will be creating such things in future chapters though, and it's important to test these functions using a server. If you are creating a local host Web, FrontPage Personal Web Server will allow you to test these functions.

▶ **❶** Make sure all your work is saved in FrontPage Editor and FrontPage Explorer and close both programs. Check your Windows program bar (at the bottom of your screen) to see if FrontPage Personal Web Server is running. If it isn't, double-click on the Fpserver icon in the FrontPage 97 folder of the Windows Explorer.

TIP SHEET

▸ **If you have been creating a Web site on a remote server, you can still test your Web pages with Internet Explorer or Netscape Navigator, but you won't need to have FrontPage Personal Web Server running to do so. Just enter your Web site's URL into the URL box in your browser, and your page should appear.**

▸ **Microsoft Internet Explorer and Netscape Navigator are the two browsers that you will see mentioned throughout this book. But there are a number of other good browsers available.**

▸ **You may notice that Internet Explorer loads your local Web pages more quickly than Netscape Navigator.**

2 The FrontPage Personal Web Server should now be running (although it is probably minimized). To see the Personal Web Server, select its button from the Program bar at the bottom of your screen. The Personal Web Server window has some bright graphics and two menus: File and Help. The File menu allows you to close the FrontPage Personal Web Server and the Help menu tells you what version of the Server is running. There really isn't anything you can do with the FrontPage Personal Web Server other than run a browser to test your Web site.

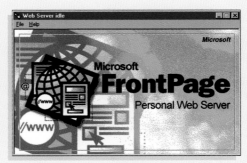

3 Click on the Preview in Browser button in the toolbar to open Microsoft Internet Explorer or Netscape Navigator, whichever browser you have installed.

4 Your page should appear in your browser, just as it will to anyone who visits your site on the Web.

How to Use Server Administrator to Administer Your Web Site

I f you're creating a Web site locally rather than on a remote server, you may want to check your Personal Web Server configuration, and you may want to set permissions for Web page authoring on the specified server. This is done using Server Administrator, a utility that comes with Microsoft FrontPage. If everything you are trying to do with FrontPage Explorer and Editor is already working, you may not need to do anything with Server Administrator.

Microsoft FrontPage installs Server Extensions which allow the Personal Web Server to serve up Web pages that are fully functional. As the Internet develops and more functionality is added to Web pages, you may need to download new Server Extensions from the Microsoft FrontPage Web site and install them. The Server Administrator is what allows you to do this.

1 From your Run menu, start the Microsoft FrontPage Server Administrator program, fpsrvwin.

5 Finally, the Security button allows you to create new Administrator user names and passwords. This topic will be covered in Chapter 20.

TIP SHEET

▶ **If you do have to install or upgrade your Server Extensions, you will be prompted for "Server Config". Your default server configuration is normally located in the file: c:\FrontPage Webs\Server\conf\httpd.cnf. Browse until you find this file and then click on OK.**

2 The Server Administrator window will be displayed. From this window you can see what settings are currently active for the Personal Web Server. If you click on the button labeled Check, the Administrator will check the current settings to make sure that they are working.

3 If you need to install or upgrade to new Server Extensions for FrontPage, you can click on the Install button and be guided through the process. If you wish to uninstall Server Extensions, click on the Uninstall button.

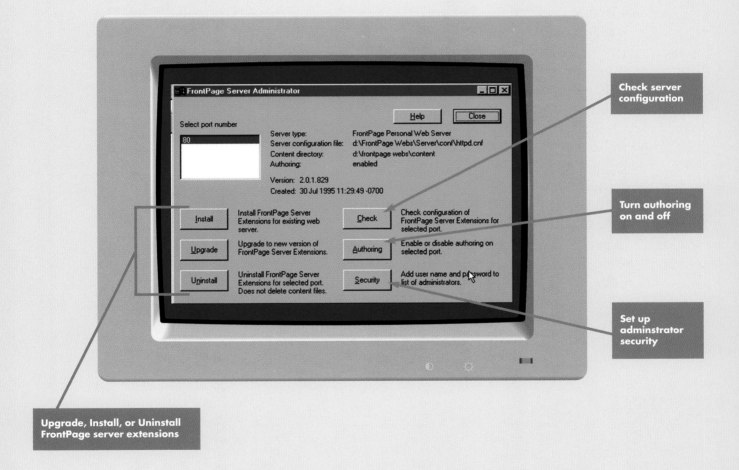

Check server configuration

Turn authoring on and off

Set up adminstrator security

Upgrade, Install, or Uninstall FrontPage server extensions

4 The Authoring button is a toggle that allows you to determine whether authoring should be allowed on your Personal Web. If you don't want any changes made on the Webs contained in the Personal Web Server, you can toggle authoring off so that no one can edit any of the pages.

CHAPTER 3

Creating a Web Page with FrontPage Editor

In Chapters 1 and 2, you had a chance to become familiar with all of the components of Microsoft FrontPage. And you created a Web site as well as a Web page. However, your Web page so far is blank, and that's no good to anyone! In this very important chapter, you'll learn the basics of adding text to your Web page. You don't want your Web page to be boring, so you'll also learn how to format the text, and how to delete and replace text when you change your mind about what you want to write.

In Chapter 2 you did a simple save on your Web page so that you could look at it in your Web browser. In this chapter you'll learn about the various options associated with saving a Web page.

How to Place a Heading on Your Web Page

Although headings aren't necessary on a Web page, they are helpful in indicating to users what the page is all about. Unless you want the subject of your Web page to be a mystery to the people who visit it, you'll probably want to create a heading. There are two ways to go about adding a heading to your page: the right way and the wrong way. The right way to add a heading is described on this page. The wrong way to create a heading is to just type some words into the top of your Web page. You'll see why this is wrong as you read on.

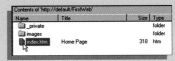

❶ If you don't already have FrontPage Explorer open, you'll have to launch it and open your Web site. Refer to Chapter 2 if you can't remember how to do this. Once you have your Web site open in Explorer, switch to FrontPage Editor by double-clicking on the page you see in either Folder or Hyperlink view.

❻ When you've entered as many heading levels as you like, save your Web page and load it into your browser to view it. Refer to Chapter 2 for details on how to do this.

❺ If you want to enter other levels of headings, you can follow the same procedure, except that you choose different heading levels (1 to 6) from the Heading sub-menu.

2 When FrontPage Editor opens up, place your cursor into the main area of the window. A vertical insertion bar will appear on the page to indicate that you can now enter text. If you don't have any text on your page, type some. Pull down the Change Style list in the Format toolbar of the FrontPage Editor and select Heading 1.

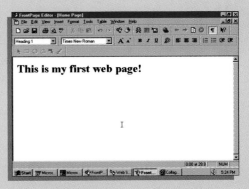

3 The text will now appear with the large type font used for Heading 1 text. Normally Heading 1 text is 36 points.

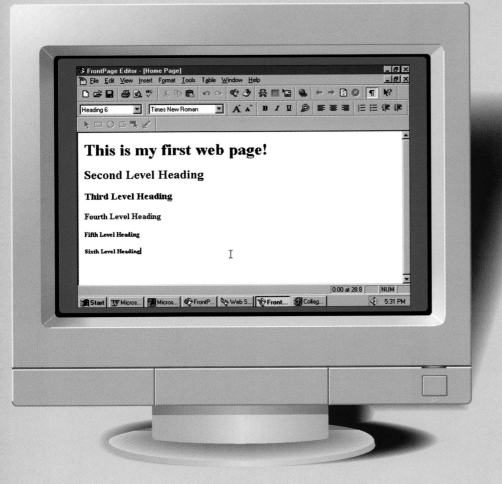

4 To turn the heading style off, you can pull down the Change Style list again, and then select Normal from the list. The text line will be short again.

How to Place Text on Your Web Page

Even though it's the graphics and all of the pretty colors that actually draw people to the World Wide Web, it's generally the text that keeps visitors at a page reading. A good combination of graphics and text is the thing to strive for. Graphics are more complicated and are covered in a later chapter. For now, it's important to figure out the basics of entering text into your Web page.

▶ **1** Open your Web site in FrontPage Explorer. Double-click on the page showing in either view to get to FrontPage Editor.

6 FrontPage Editor will check the spelling of all of the text you have entered. The Spelling dialog box will appear and will alert you to any words that are not in the dictionary. If the word it finds is something that wouldn't be in a dictionary anyway, such as your name, click on Ignore. If a word is spelled incorrectly, pick the correct spelling from the Suggestions list and click on the Change button. When the spell check is complete, save your Web page.

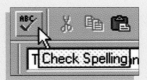

 5 When you've finished typing in all of your text, click on the spell-check button on the toolbar.

TIP SHEET

▶ As with any electronic text document, typos can happen! Make sure you use the spell-checker before you put your Web documents in the public domain — it may prevent some embarrassment.

2 To enter text into your Web page place your insertion point where you want to place the text and then select Normal from the Change Style list.

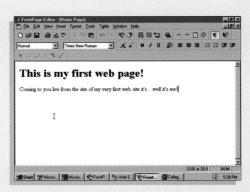

3 A text cursor will appear in the window and you can start typing. An even easier way to enter text is to simply place your cursor on the Web page and then start typing.

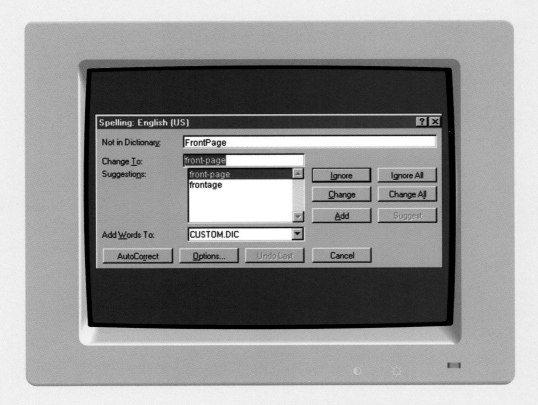

4 You can type as much text as you like, and FrontPage Editor will word-wrap for you. If you finish a few sentences and you want to start a new paragraph, simply hit the Enter key. FrontPage Editor will move your cursor down to a new paragraph.

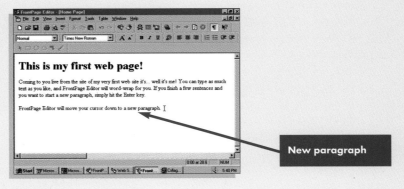

New paragraph

How to Edit Your Text

Like many great works, a Web page is often a work in progress. Just because you place your Web page on a server where people can see it doesn't mean that it won't ever change. Anyway, you will often want to change the text that you enter. This page contains a number of tips and tricks for deleting, copying, and moving text around. Because cutting and pasting are used so often there are many tips for performing these tasks quickly. Knowing these tricks can make your Web page editing go much faster.

TIP SHEET

▶ In addition to using the cut, copy, and paste options from the Edit menu, you can also use some shortcut keys. Try Ctrl+C for copy, Ctrl+X for cut, and Ctrl+V for paste.

▶ If you wanted to edit all of the text on your current Web page (if you wanted to copy it to the Clipboard to paste it into another application), choose Select All from the Edit menu. Then you can edit all of the text at once.

▶ The cut, copy, and paste options are also available from the pop-up menu that appears when you right-click with your mouse on highlighted text.

▶ Yet another way to cut, copy, and paste is to use the cut, copy, and paste buttons on the toolbar. The cut icon is a pair of scissors, the copy icon is two sheets, and the paste icon is a clipboard and a sheet.

▶ In FrontPage Editor, open a Web page on which you have text that you want to change. You can do this by double-clicking on that page's icon in the FrontPage Explorer.

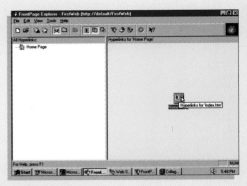

▶ **1** In FrontPage Editor, open a Web page on which you have text that you want to change. You can do this by double-clicking on that page's icon in either view of FrontPage Explorer.

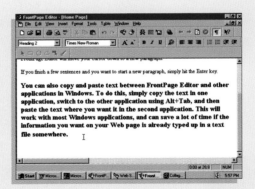

6 You can also copy and paste text between FrontPage Editor and other applications in Windows. To do this, simply copy the text in one application, switch to the other application using Alt+Tab, and then paste the text where you want it in the second application. This will work with most Windows applications, and can save a lot of time if the information you want on your Web page is already typed up in a text file somewhere.

2 To delete text from your Web page, highlight the text and then press the delete key on your keyboard, or choose Clear from the Edit menu. You will be able to get this text back by choosing Undo from the Edit menu.

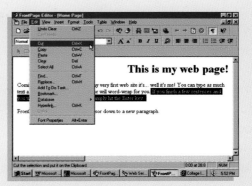

3 If you want to move text from one spot to another on your Web page, highlight the text and then select Cut from the Edit menu. The text will disappear.

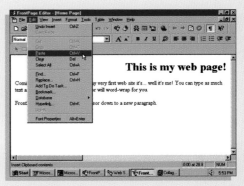

4 Move your cursor to the spot where you want the text to be inserted and choose Paste from the Edit menu. The text will reappear there.

5 If you want to copy text from one spot to another, highlight the text and then select Copy from the Edit menu. Move your cursor to the spot where you want the text to be repeated and then select Paste from the Edit menu.

How to Change Text Style

Normal text in FrontPage Editor is left-aligned, and will generally show up in a Web browser as something that looks like 12-point Times New Roman font. However, your text doesn't always have to look that way. You can have text that is centered or right-aligned, that is a larger or smaller font, or that is bolded, underlined, or italicized. You can also assign different fonts to your text. Adding characteristics such as these can really help to make your content stand out.

▶ **1** In FrontPage Editor, open a Web page that has text already typed on it.

6 You can edit text font by selecting Font from the Format menu. The Font dialog box will appear. You can select font type, style, size, effect, and color in this dialog box. In the Special Styles tab you can select blinking, strike-through, and a number of other styles.

2 To change your text style, highlight the text that you want to change and click on the appropriate button on the toolbar. To make text bold, click on the **B** button, to italicize, click on the *I* button and to underline, click on the U button.

3 To increase the text size of highlighted text, click on the Increase Font button, which is an A with an up arrow beside it. To decrease font size, click on the Decrease Font button, which is an A with a down arrow beside it.

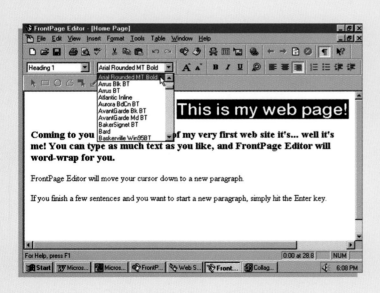

5 To change text font, select the text and choose a font from the Change Font list in the Formatting toolbar.

4 If you want a paragraph to be centered on the page, place your insertion point within the paragraph and click on the Centering button on the toolbar. If you want a paragraph to be aligned to the right margin, place your insertion point in the paragraph and click on the Right-Align button on the toolbar.

How to Save Your Web Page

In Chapter 2, you saved your Web page so that you could look at it in your Web browser. However, there are a number of different options and choices involved in saving a Web page, and before you go any further in developing your Web site, you should learn about these.

There are three save options under the File menu, and this page will show you what the difference is between the three.

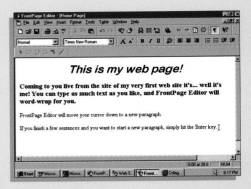
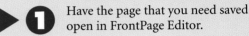

▶ **1** Have the page that you need saved open in FrontPage Editor.

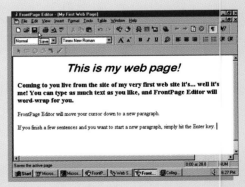

6 If you've already saved a Web page, but you've made changes and you want to save it again, simply choose Save from the File menu or click on the Save button on the toolbar.

TIP SHEET

▶ You can save your Web page as a Web page, as a template, and as a file on your hard disk. The default option is to save your Web page as a Web page, specifying a URL and a title. This is what you'll want to do most of the time.

▶ When you type in the URL for your Web page, the URL can't have any spaces, and must end in .htm (or .html if you are putting your page on a UNIX server).

▶ Another option in the File menu is the Save All option. This will save every Web page that you have open in FrontPage Editor (so that you don't have to save each individually).

▶ If you don't understand the templates stuff, don't worry, this is described in more detail in Chapter 9.

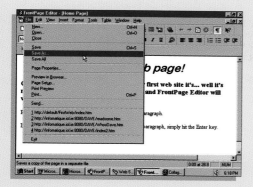

2 If you are saving your Web page for the first time, choose Save As from the File menu.

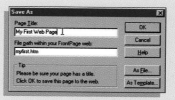

3 The Save As dialog box will appear. The default title is "HomePage" and the default URL (Web file name) is index.htm. Give your page a title. Notice that as you type in a title, FrontPage Editor attempts to make the URL out of that title. You can accept the URL that FrontPage Editor creates, or you can change it. At this point if you click on OK, the Web page will be saved as a Web page within the Web you currently have open in FrontPage Explorer.

4 There are two more options in the Save As dialog box. You can save the current Web page as a template — this means that you'll be able to use that Web page later on as a template for creating other pages. To do this, click on the As Template button in the Save As dialog box. The Save As Template dialog box will open. This gives the same options as the Save As dialog box, except that you also get to type in a description. When you browse through the templates later on, this description would show for this template.

5 Another option is to save your Web page as a file. To do this, click on the As File button in the Save As dialog box. This will bring up a normal Windows Save As dialog box. You shouldn't use this option normally — only use this when you need a second copy of your page on disk.

TRY IT!

By now you've been introduced to all of the components of Microsoft FrontPage Explorer. You've read about how to initialize your Web site, how to create a Web page and put text on it, and how to test that Web page. Now let's try out what you've learned.

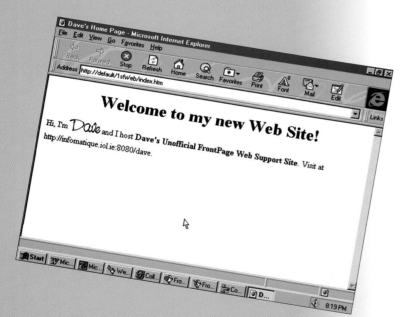

1

Launch FrontPage.

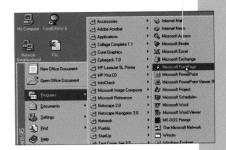

2

Select From a Wizard or Template in the Getting Started dialog box. Click OK in the dialog box.

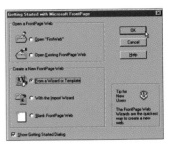

3

In the New FrontPage Web dialog box, highlight Normal Web and hit the OK button.

In the Normal Web Template dialog box, type in default as the Web Server and type in FirstWeb for the name of your Web site. Then click OK.

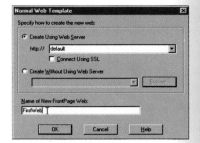

In the Name and Password Required dialog box, type in the name and password that you gave when you installed Microsoft FrontPage. Keep in mind that passwords are case-sensitive. Then click OK.

You'll see your new Web in FrontPage Explorer, with a page in it called Home Page.

Now you'll want to edit Normal Page to make it into your own personalized Web page. To launch FrontPage Editor, double-click on the Home Page icon in the Hyperlink view of FrontPage Explorer.

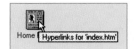

When FrontPage Editor appears with Home Page open, you'll want to give it your own title. Click on Save As in the File menu.

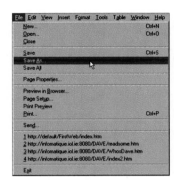

In the Save As dialog box, change the name to Jane's Home Page (but insert your own name!). Then click OK.

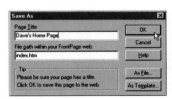

Now you will want to put a heading into your Web page. From the Change Style list in the Format toolbar, select Heading 1.

Continue to next page ▶

TRY IT!

Continue
below

13

Type in a
paragraph
about your-
self.

11

Type in a
heading for
your page.

14

Highlight
some of the
outstanding
facts about
yourself and
then click on
the bold but-
ton on the
toolbar.

15

Click on your
heading and
then click on
the centering
button on the
toolbar.

12

Press Enter.
Your cursor
will move
down to the
next para-
graph, and
the style will
revert to
Normal

16

Highlight
your name
and choose a
new font from
the Change
Font list.

17

Click on the Increase Font button once, to make your name bigger.

18

Click on the Spell Check button on the toolbar. Either accept the spelling corrections suggested, or ignore them if the words are spelled correctly but not recognized. When the spell check is finished, click OK when you get the FrontPage Editor alert about it.

19

Save the changes you have made to your page by clicking on the Save button on the toolbar.

20

Click on the Preview in Browser button in the FrontPage Editor toolbar.

21

View your site in your Web browser. Your Web page should appear! Congratulations — you've just created and tested your first Web site and Web page.

22

Note any changes you want to make on your page when you return to the FrontPage Editor.

23

Exit your Internet browser.

CHAPTER 4

Adding Lists to Your Page

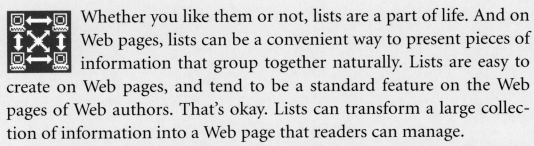 Whether you like them or not, lists are a part of life. And on Web pages, lists can be a convenient way to present pieces of information that group together naturally. Lists are easy to create on Web pages, and tend to be a standard feature on the Web pages of Web authors. That's okay. Lists can transform a large collection of information into a Web page that readers can manage.

Lists shouldn't be overused. A Web page that consists of one long list looks boring, and probably won't do much to catch your reader's eye. However, when used in moderation, lists can really help you to organize your content. For now, you should get to know how to add and edit a basic list on your Web page.

How to Place Lists on Your Web Page

If you've ever created a list in a word processing program, you know that bullets can help make a list stand out. The same idea applies to Web pages. Bulleted lists are really easy to produce with FrontPage Editor.

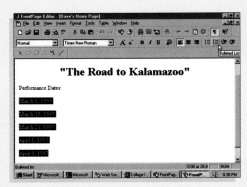

▶ **1** If you already have a list of items typed into your Web page, but you want them formatted to look like a list rather than a bunch of separate lines, the steps are easy. Highlight the items, and then click on the Bulleted List button on the FrontPage Editor toolbar.

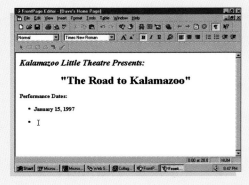

5 A bullet will appear on the page, and you can type in your first item. Press Enter when you are finished and another bullet will appear. Enter all of your list items and then press the Enter key twice to get to a new paragraph.

TIP SHEET

▶ You may have noticed that in the Change Style List there are four choices: Bulleted, Numbered, Directory, and Menu. You'll learn how to create numbered lists later in this chapter. You don't need to worry about menu and directory lists. These are non-conventional HTML tags that many browsers won't recognize. Even FrontPage Editor doesn't display directory and menu lists any differently than bulleted lists. Maybe these will be used in the future though, so tuck those names away in the back of your mind!

2 Your list will be formatted with bullets. If you want to add another item to your list, simply put your cursor at the end of the last item, and press enter. A new bullet will appear and you can type your new entry.

- April 1, 1997
- April 4, 1997
- | I

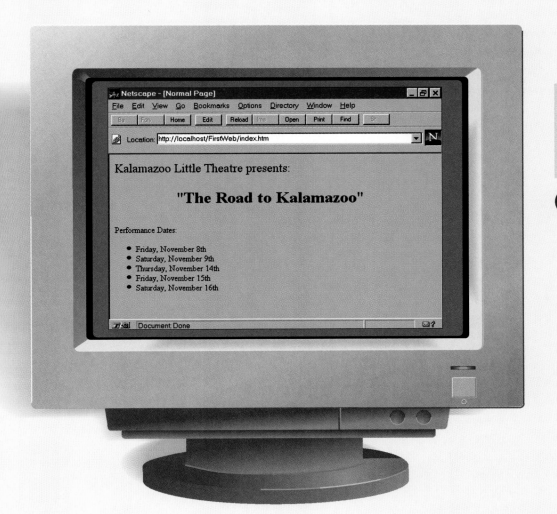

- March 21, 1997
- April 1, 1997
- April 4, 1997

| I

3 When you've finished adding items to your bulleted list, press Enter. Your cursor will move down to the next line and another bullet will appear. If you press Enter again, the bullet will disappear and your cursor will move down to a new paragraph.

4 If you haven't typed your list into your Web page at all, then you can use a different approach to creating a bulleted list. With your cursor placed where you want to put a list, select Bulleted List from the Change Style list

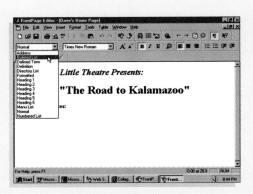

How to Organize Lists

When you need to present a lot of related data, a simple list may not do the trick. For example, if you've got data that has a hierarchical organization, nested lists may be the only accurate method of presentation.

On this page, you'll learn how to nest lists within lists, and how to edit lists that you've already created.

► **1** A play synopsis is fairly structured — you have a few acts and within each act you have a number of scenes. This is a perfect example for nested lists. Type in the first level of data, in this case, the title of each act. Highlight all of these and then format them as a bulleted list.

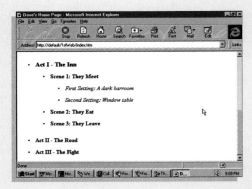

6 You should be aware that the different bullet styles that show up in FrontPage Editor are not necessarily what will be seen in a browser. It's always a good idea to use the Preview in Browser button to see exactly how your list will look in your own browser.

TIP SHEET

▶ **A quick way to end a nested list is to press Ctrl+End. This will move your cursor to the bottom of the page.**

▶ **Try to make sure that you format the text in your list so that the formatting is consistent for each nesting level. A poorly formatted list can look very unprofessional.**

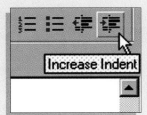

2 Place your cursor at the end of the first item. Press Enter. A new bullet will appear Then click twice on the Increase Indent button in the Format toolbar, You can type in your second-level information, in this case the scene title. If you want to enter more than one second-level list item, press Enter after typing in the first and you'll get another bullet.

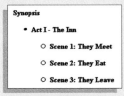

3 When you've completed your first nested list, go on to the next first-level list item and repeat the procedure to enter another nested list.

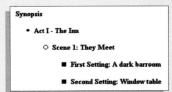

4 You can have nested lists within nested lists, within nested lists within nested lists — you get the idea. To achieve this, repeat the procedure above, except start by placing your cursor at the end of a nested list item. You'll end up with a bullet that is twice indented from your original margin — a third level listing.

5 Your nested lists can be made even easier to read by formatting the different levels. You do this by simply selecting the text you want to format and then clicking on whatever formatting buttons you like. For example, you could make all the second-level nested items italic, and you could decrease the font size of all the third-level nested items. To remove text formatting, simply highlight the text and click on the format button again.

How to Create and Edit Numbered Lists

S ome lists, by their very content, need to be numbered. A good example of a numbered list is a set of procedural instructions for completing a task, especially if the order of execution is important.

On this page, you'll learn how to create a numbered list. You'll also learn how to format a nested numbered list to suit your purposes.

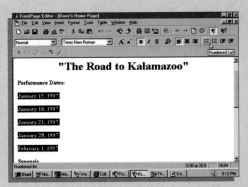

1 If you already have a bulleted list on your page, or if you have several items listed (but not formatted into a list) on your page, you can make these into a numbered list. Simply highlight the items and then click on the numbered list button on the FrontPage Editor toolbar.

5 Select Bullets and Numbering from the Format menu to make a nested, numbered list that will not start over at '1.' The Start At spin box lets you define a starting number for your list other than '1'.

 If you haven't yet typed in the items you want to make into a numbered list, start by placing your cursor in the spot you want the list to appear. Then select List from the FrontPage Editor Insert menu, and from the sub-menu select Numbered.

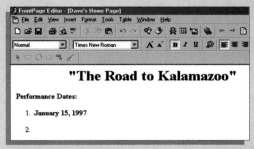

 The number '1' will appear on the page, and you can type in your first item. If you press Enter, the number '2' will appear and you can type in your second item. When you have typed in all of your items, press the Enter key twice.

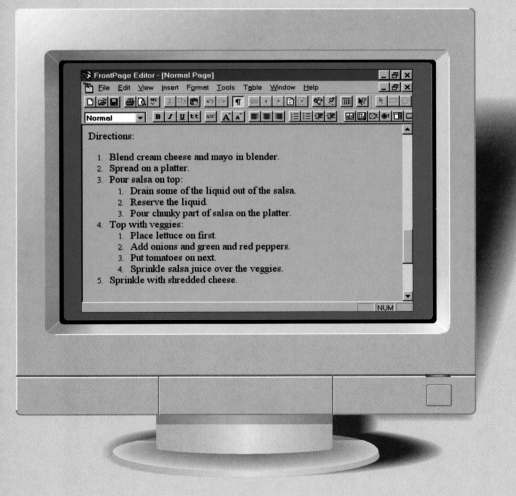

When you nest a numbered list within a numbered list, the numbering starts over again. So, if you create a numbered list, nested underneath item number '1,' you'll get another (further indented) item number '1.'

How to Create Definition Lists

A definition list is a list of two-part items. The first part of an item is listed against the left margin, and the second part of the item is listed right underneath the first part, but indented slightly.

Definition lists work perfectly for glossaries. Another good use of definition lists is for bibliographic-style listings. And they are ideal for lists of terms for which you are providing definitions. You may not have any need to create a definition list at this point, but you should learn how to create such a listing, so that when you do need to create one, you'll already know how.

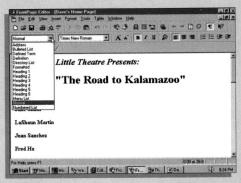

▶ **1** The easiest way to create a definition list is to type in all of the terms you want defined, following each with its definition on the next line. Click on the first term. Click on the down arrow of the Change Style list.

7 You can change a defined term to a definition. Highlight it and then choose Definition from the Change Style list.

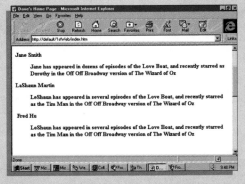

6 Press the Enter key and type in your new term. Then, press the Enter key again and type in the definition.

TIP SHEET

▶ Definition lists don't tend to nest well within other definition lists. However, they can look okay if nested within a regular bulleted or numbered list.

▶ Don't forget that definition lists can be formatted with bolding, italics, font sizes, and anything else that can be done to regular text. Just make sure your formatting is consistent.

2 Select Defined Term from the Change Style list. Your term is now formatted as a defined term, although it won't look any different.

3 Next, select the definition for the term you just formatted. From the same list, select Definition. The definition will now appear indented from the term, and it will be right underneath the term, with little space between the two.

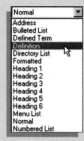

4 Repeat the procedure until all of your terms and definitions have been formatted.

5 If you already have a definition list, and you want to add another definition, place your cursor at the left margin, at the beginning of the defined term which you want following the term you are inserting.

Jane Smith
   Jane has appeared in dozens of episodes of the Love Boat, and recently
   starred as Dorothy in the Off Off Broadway version of The Wizard of Oz
LaShaun Martin
   LeShaun has appeared in several episodes of the Love Boat, and recently
   starred as the Tim Man in the Off Off Broadway version of The Wizard of Oz
 Fred Hu

   LeShaun has appeared in several episodes of the Love Boat, and recently
   starred as the Tim Man in the Off Off Broadway version of The Wizard of Oz

CHAPTER 5:

Placing Tables on Your Web Page

Tables can be a great way to organize information on your Web page, and they can actually save you space if your Web page is already getting to be too long. Traditionally, creating tables in HTML has been a cumbersome process. However, the ability to place text and graphics side by side on a page, and to present information in columns and rows makes using tables almost a necessity on some pages. FrontPage Editor uses the table menus that can be found in Microsoft Word, so anyone who is familiar with creating a table in a Word document will find it really easy to create a table on a Web page.

It's important to have a good idea of what your table should look like before you start trying to create one in FrontPage Editor. If you sketch out your table on paper first and keep that paper handy for quick reference, you'll save yourself a lot of time.

How to Define a Table for Your Web Page

Creating and editing tables in FrontPage Editor is easy. Editing a table basically consists of one big step—filling out the values in the Insert Table dialog box. There are a lot of different parameters that you can set to make your table look exactly the way you want it to. On this page you'll get a detailed tour of this dialog box.

1 With a Web page open in FrontPage Editor, click on the Insert Table button in the FrontPage toolbar.

► When you specify number of columns and rows, don't forget to count your table headings as a row also!

► When you type in values for the table parameters, don't get stressed out trying to pick the exact values you need; you can come back and change these values later if you don't like the look of your table.

► You should try to specify the width of your table in percent rather than in pixels because that way when the user re-sizes the browser window, the table will adjust so that it still fits well on the screen. If you don't select the Width check box at all, the browser will make the table as wide as necessary to accommodate the cell contents.

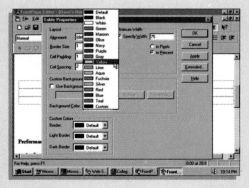

6 You can define background colors for your Table, Border, Light Border, and Dark Border in your table by selecting colors in the Custom Background area of the Table Properties dialog box. When you've chosen all your parameters, click OK and your table will appear on your Web page.

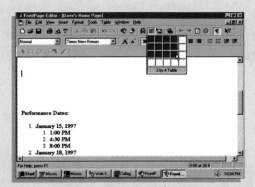

2 Click and drag in the grid that appears to define the number of rows and columns you wish to have in your table. A table appears that spans the width of your screen, with the number of rows and columns you selected.

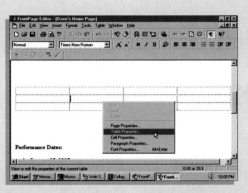

3 To edit the properties of the table you just created, right click on the table and select Table Properties from the shortcut menu.

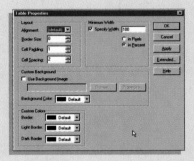

4 The Layout area of the Table Properties dialog box allows you to set Alignment, Border Size, Cell Padding, and Cell Spacing. *Alignment* specifies whether the table will be in the center of your Web page, at the left margin, or at the right margin. If you leave this parameter as "default," the table will default to your paragraph alignment. The *Border Size* parameter specifies the width, in pixels, of the border you put around your table. If you don't want a visible border around your table, select 0. The *Cell Padding* parameter specifies the amount of space, in pixels, between the contents of each table cell and the cell wall. Finally, the *Cell Spacing* parameter specifies, in pixels, how much space should be left between adjacent table cells.

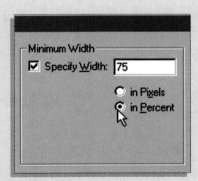

5 The Minimum Width section of the Insert Table dialog box contains the width specifications. You can specify how wide your table will be in two ways. If you select the In Pixels radio button, then the number specified in the Width box above will be the width of your table in pixels, no matter how big the user's browser window is. If you pick the In Percent radio button, your table will be the specified percentage width with respect to the browser window.

How to Change Table Format

When you use the Insert Table dialog box to define your table, you'll notice that what you get is a perfect grid. If you specified three rows and three columns, then you'll get nine cells. But what if you want one of the cells in the first row to span over two or more columns? And what if you want one of the cells in a column to span two or more rows? Special formatting like this can easily be achieved in FrontPage, and on this page you'll learn how.

▶ **1** In FrontPage Editor, open the page on which you've inserted a table. It doesn't matter if the table has text or other contents, or if the table is empty.

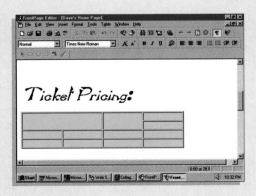

5 You may also end up with more rows than you had originally planned for. On the following page you'll find out how to delete those rows.

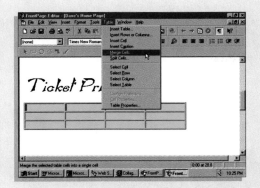

2 To make a table cell span more than one column, select all of the table cells in that row, spanning those columns. This is the most difficult step if your table is empty. To select two adjacent empty cells, place your cursor in the first and then, holding your mouse button down, place your cursor in the next cell. The first cell will look highlighted and the second cell won't. But that's okay. From the Table menu, select Merge Cells. The two cells will have become one larger cell.

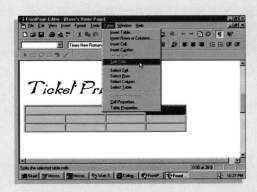

3 If you want to make a cell span two or more rows, split the adjacent cells up into the number of rows you want that cell to span. Put your cursor in a cell in the same row as the cell you want spanning a few rows. Choose Select Cell from the Table menu. Then choose Split Cells from the Table menu.

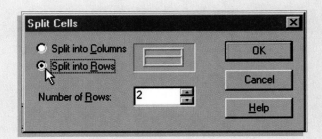

4 The Split Cells dialog box will appear. Choose Split into Rows. Then type in the number of rows that you want your original cell to span. Click on OK.

How to Add and Delete Columns and Rows

S ometimes you'll realize halfway through adding text to a table that you need to add another column or that you've got an extra row you don't need. This isn't a big problem. FrontPage Editor makes it simple to add or delete rows and columns.

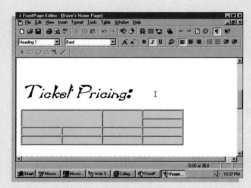

1 Open a Web page with a table on it in FrontPage Editor.

8 When the new column is added to your table, it will appear small. However, when you start entering text into it, the column (and table) will expand in width.

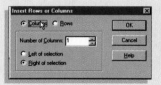

7 The Insert Rows or Columns dialog box will appear. Select Insert Columns and then type in the Number of Columns you want added. Select either Left of Selection or Right of Selection to indicate where you want the column(s) inserted. Click OK and the extra columns will appear in your table.

TIP SHEET

▶ **The easiest way to select a row or a column is to put your cursor right over the edge of the table near the column or row you want selected. You can also place your cursor in a column or row, and se- lect that column or row using the Table menu.**

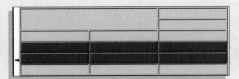

2 To delete a row, select the row you want deleted by placing your cursor to the left of the row, until the cursor turns into a small black arrow pointing right. You can click and drag down to select more than one row to delete. Then press the Delete key.

3 To delete a column, place your cursor just above the column until it turns into a small down-pointing arrow. Then press the Delete key.

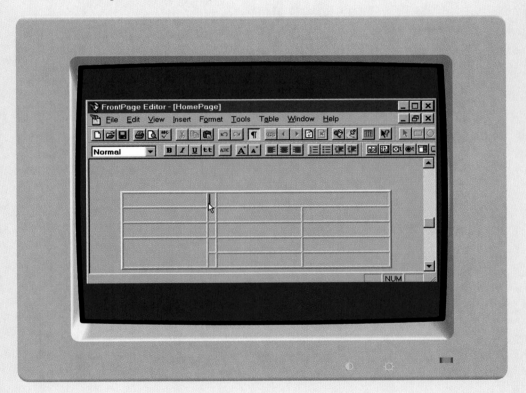

4 To add a row or rows, put your cursor in a cell above or below where you want to add the row. Then select Insert Rows or Columns from the Table menu.

6 To add a column or columns, put your cursor in a cell beside where you want to add the column. Then select Insert Rows or Columns from the Table menu.

5 The Insert Rows or Columns dialog box will appear. Select Insert Rows and then type in the number of rows you want added. Select either Above Selection or Below Selection to indicate where you want the rows inserted. Click OK and the extra rows will appear in your table.

How to Place Text in a Table

You can put lots of different things into the cell of a table on a Web page. Later on in Chapter 11 you'll learn about pictures, and you'll be able to put these into a table cell. You can also put hyperlinks (which you'll learn about in Chapter 8) into table cells.

However, almost every table you see on the World Wide Web will have at least some text in it. So, before you go on to all the fancy stuff, you should learn how to add text to a table.

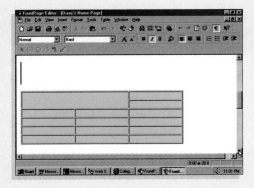

 1 Open your Web page in FrontPage Editor and scroll down to a table you've inserted.

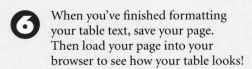 **6** When you've finished formatting your table text, save your page. Then load your page into your browser to see how your table looks!

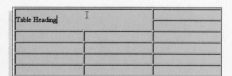

2 To add text to your table, simply place your cursor in the cell you want the text to be in and then start typing.

Heading

3 All table cells in a column or row will expand to fit the largest word you type into the cell.

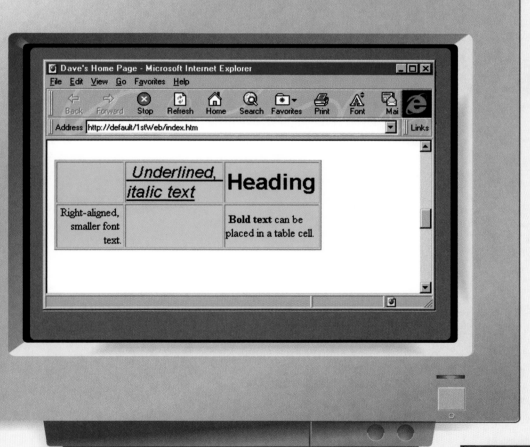

4 Notice that if you type lots of text into a cell, so that the text has to continue on to new lines, the height of all the cells in that row will expand simultaneously.

5 You can format the text you put into a table cell, simply by highlighting it and then clicking on any of the formatting buttons on the toolbar. You can center or right-align text; you can bold, italicize, or underline text, and you can change text size.

TRY IT!

It's time again to put the skills you've learned to use. You may have noticed that the pages used as examples in Chapter 4 were for a Little Theater Company. Your job right now is to create a Web page for the Bartica Little Theater Company. In the past two chapters you learned how to create and use lists and tables. You'll get a chance to use both of these skills as you put together a Web page for the Bartica Little Theater's newest production — Romeo and Juliet.

Launch FrontPage 97.

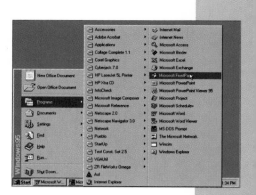

In the
FrontPage
Explorer,
open the Web
you created in
the last Try It
section by clicking on the Web name in
the file menu.

Enter the
password you
use to access
the Web.

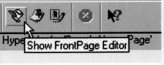

After the Web
appears, click
on the FrontPage Editor button on the
toolbar.

In FrontPage
Editor, select
New from the
file menu.

In the New
Page dialog
box, make
sure that
Normal Page
is highlighted
and then click on OK.

A blank page
will be open
in FrontPage
Editor now.
Type in a few
lines to intro-
duce the play.

Format the
introduction
and the play
title by
changing
fonts and
alignment.

Type in a list of performance dates for
Romeo and Juliet.

Continue to next page ▶

TRY IT!

Continue below

10 Highlight the list of dates and click on the Bulleted List button on the toolbar.

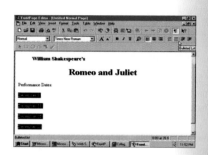

11 You'll want to include the cast list on the Web page, and this is a perfect opportunity to use a definition list. Type in the name of each character in the play, and on the following line, type the name of the actor who plays that character.

12 Highlight the first character name, and then select Defined Term from the Change Style list.

13 Highlight the actor's name now and select Definition from the Change Style list.

14 Repeat this procedure for each character and actor.

15 Now the Little Theater wants you to include a table showing the seating options, along with the ticket prices for each seat. You should design your table on a piece of paper before you try to create in FrontPage Editor. You'll want three columns and four rows.

In FrontPage Editor, put your cursor where you want the table to appear. Click on the Insert Table button. Click and drag in the table grid to define a table with 3 rows and 4 columns.

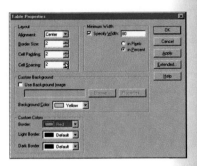

Right-click on the new table and select Table Properties from the shortcut menu. Then, set the Alignment to Center — this centers the table in the middle of the page. Type 2 in the Border Size box. Type 2 in the Cell Padding box. Leave the Cell Spacing number as 2 — this will put two pixels of space between adjacent cells. In the Specify Width part of the Insert Table dialog box, make sure that "in Percent" is selected, and type 80 in the Specify Width box. This will make the table take up 80 percent of the width of a browser window. Set the background color to yellow and the border color to red. Finally, click on OK.

You will now have an empty table on your Web page. Place your cursor in the first cell and type in Seating Type.

Delete the fourth column from your table. Then type appropriate information into the rest of the table cells. The cells will expand as necessary to accommodate the amount of text you wish to include.

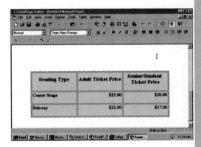

You can now format the contents of the cells as you would any other text — simply highlight the text you want to format and then click on the necessary toolbar buttons.

Save your new Web page and open it up in your browser to see what it looks like.

CHAPTER 6

Getting Input from Your Visitors

 If you've spent lots of time cruising the World Wide Web, then you know that forms are an integral part of many types of Web pages. Forms can be used for getting feedback about the page itself from page visitors. Forms can also be used for search queries or for surveys. Most important, though, forms are used for commercial purposes. If you ever try to buy anything online, you'll definitely be filling out an online form.

Creating forms and gathering data from those forms is quite a complex task if you're just writing raw HTML. When you create forms with Microsoft FrontPage, you don't have to worry about learning any computer scripting languages. All you have to do is follow the instructions in the next two chapters and let FrontPage do the rest!

In this chapter we will look at creating the form for your Web page. In Chapter 7 you'll learn how to get FrontPage to collect the data that people will enter into your forms.

How to Get Input through Check Boxes

The check box is probably the easiest form element to create. And check boxes are the best way to get a Yes or No answer from your audience. Check boxes can also be used for those lists where you want the user to check all items that apply.

1 In FrontPage Editor, open a new page by selecting New from the File menu and choosing the Normal Page template.

7 Repeat the procedure for all the items you want made into a check box. Save your page. Your form isn't complete yet. In the next chapter we'll enable the form to accept input. For now, you can save the page, load it into your browser, and try selecting one or more check boxes.

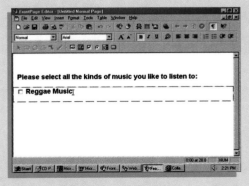

6 A check box will appear in the form outline. The cursor will be beside the check box. Type in a name to describe the check box.

TIP SHEET

▸ **When you give your check box a name in the Check Box Properties dialog box, make sure it is descriptive and at least similar to the name that you type beside the check box. When you get a file that gives you form output (you'll learn how to do this in Chapter 7), you'll want to be able to easily identify which check boxes the user actually selected.**

▸ **The initial state of a check box can be either selected or not. If you think that the option you type beside a particular check box is something that most users will select anyway, then you might want to have it checked initially, so the user has less work to do. However, this may influence the user's selection—they may leave it selected because they think that is what you want them to do. Creating unbiased forms is a subject for an entire book, and obviously can't be covered here, but put some thought into what you choose as the initial state of your check boxes.**

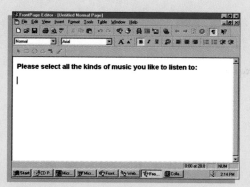

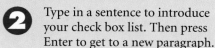

2 Type in a sentence to introduce your check box list. Then press Enter to get to a new paragraph.

3 Select Forms Toolbar from the View menu, and click on the check box icon in the Forms toolbar.

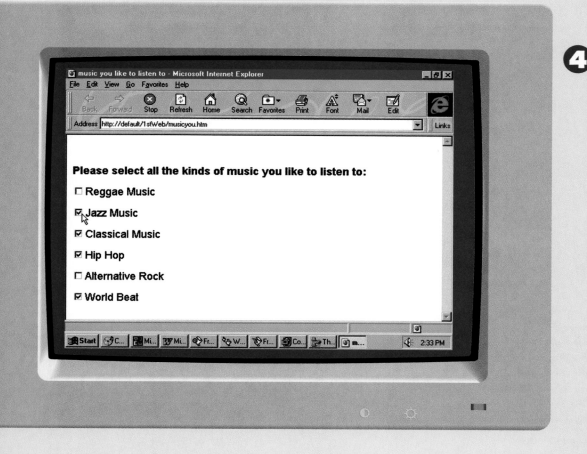

4 Double-click on the new check box on your page to open the Check Box Properties dialog box. You'll notice a dotted line on the page. This is your form outline. You'll need to enter a name for your check box—this name will show up in your data file when anyone fills in the form. The default Value is ON and the default initial state for the check box is Not Checked.

5 Enter a name for the check box value and choose an initial state — checked or not checked. Then click OK.

How to Use Radio Buttons

Radio buttons are almost identical to check boxes, except for two small differences. First of all, radio buttons are round, rather than square. More important, when users are presented with a list of radio buttons, they can only pick one item from the list. So, if they select the first item in a radio list and then they select another item in the radio list, the first item becomes unselected.

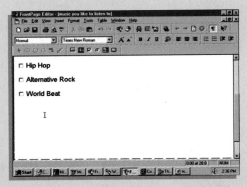

1 In FrontPage Editor, open an existing page, or create a new page. If you want to add a radio button list to a form that is already there, put your cursor inside the dotted form boundary. Otherwise, place your cursor where you want the form to appear.

8 Save your page. Even though you can't get any input from this radio button list yet, you can load it into your Web browser to see what it looks like.

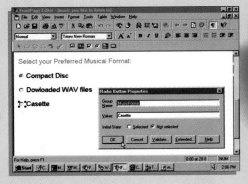
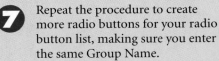

7 Repeat the procedure to create more radio buttons for your radio button list, making sure you enter the same Group Name.

TIP SHEET

▶ It is very important that you give all the radio buttons in a set the same name when you create them. If you use different names, then the browser will interpret this as two separate sets of radio buttons and the user will be able to select more than one button.

▶ When entering names into the dialog boxes for any of the form elements, you cannot include spaces. You can use mixed upper- and lowercase though, to help distinguish between words.

▶ Remember that only one radio button in your list can be selected as the initial state.

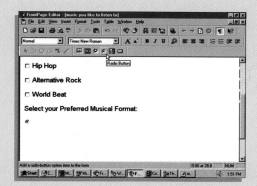

 Type in a sentence to introduce your radio button list. Press Enter. Then click on the Radio Button icon on the toolbar.

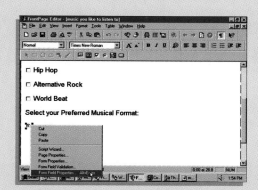

 Right-click on the radio button and select Field Properties from the shortcut menu.

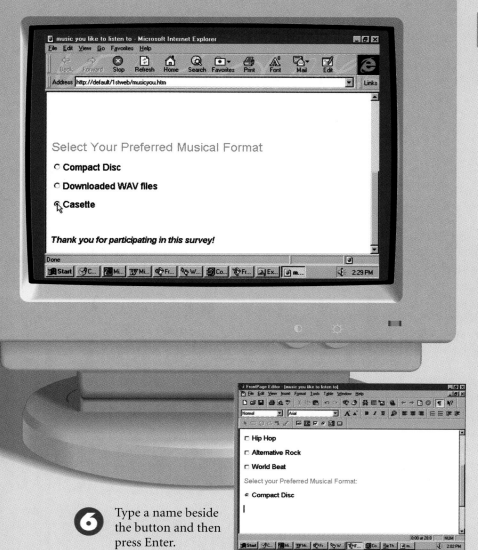

The Radio Button Properties dialog box will appear. In this dialog box, you must enter a Group Name to identify the set of radio buttons you are creating. You must also enter a name for the particular radio button you are creating. Enter this in the Value field.

Now, decide whether you want the current radio button to be selected by default. (You don't have to have any of the buttons selected by default if you don't want to.) If you want it selected, choose that option for the Initial State. Click OK to create the radio button.

Type a name beside the button and then press Enter.

How to Get Online Input

Sometimes a simple check box or radio button won't get you the information you are looking for. You'll often need to allow the user to type information into your online form. Personal profile forms, where users enter their names and other information into text boxes, are quite common on the Web. Most people will have filled one of these out when downloading software, or when registering at a Web site. If you want the people who visit your Web site to enter their names or addresses into your form, you will need to use one-line input form elements.

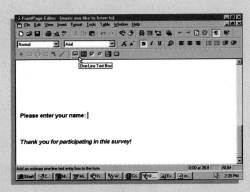

1 In FrontPage Editor, open an existing page, or create a new page. Type an introductory sentence for your text box in the spot where you want the box to appear. Then click on the One-Line Text Box button on the Forms toolbar.

7 Save your page, and check out the one-line text box in your browser.

TIP SHEET

▶ Make sure that you set the Password option to Yes if you are asking users to enter confidential information.

▶ Use the one-line form element when asking for a small amount of data, such as a name. If you want someone to enter in a paragraph about your product, or some other lengthy information, you should use a scrolling text input box. This is described on the following page.

▶ You can allow users to enter more text than is allowed by the physical length of the text box. To do this, specify the Maximum Characters field as larger than the Width in Characters field. Users will have to navigate through the one-line text box using arrow keys if they type in more text than the length of the box will display.

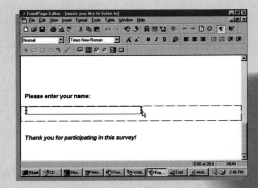

6 If the text box looks bigger or smaller than you wanted it to look, place your cursor over the edge of the box, and drag the box to make it smaller or larger.

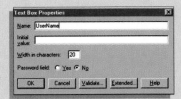

2

Double-click on the new text box. The One-Line Text Box Properties dialog box will appear. In the Name field, type in a name that will identify the data which a user enters into this one-line text box.

3

If you want to have text already in the box (which users can accept or replace), type this text into the Initial Value field.

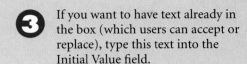

4

Specify a width in characters for the text box. This will determine how wide the box will appear in the browser.

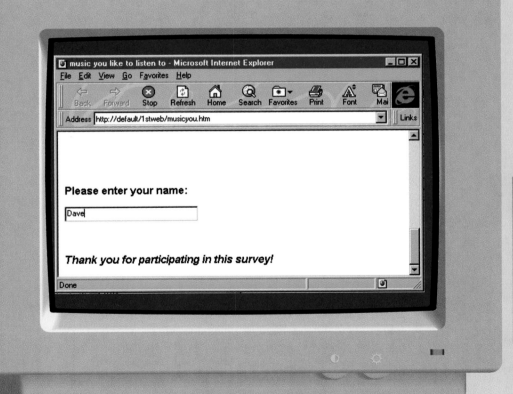

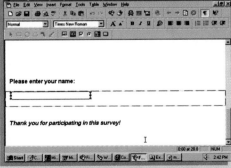

5

If you want the box to be a password box (when users type, stars will appear in the place of characters), select Yes for the Password option. Click OK. Your one-line text box will appear in FrontPage Editor.

How to Create Scrolling Text Input Boxes

If you really want people to express themselves, you've got to give them room to do so. A scrolling text input box does just that — it allows people to enter as much text as they like (well, almost). This is really handy if you're asking users to give you their opinion about something, or report a problem, or even to write you a poem.

TIP SHEET

▶ The size of a scrolling text box depends on a number of factors. If you have lots of space on your page, you can have ten lines of text as the visible height of your scroll box. If you don't have much room, make your text box only three lines high. You should never make your text box more than 80 characters wide, because users who browse at low resolution won't be able to see the whole width of the text box at once.

▶ Users will be able to enter as much text as they like into your scrolling text box. You can prevent them from doing so by using advanced HTML tags to specify a length limit on the scrolling text box, but that is too advanced to be covered here. Consult the Appendix for more information on using advanced HTML features with FrontPage.

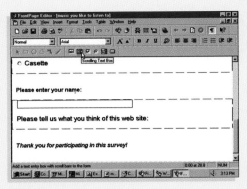

▶ **1** In FrontPage Editor, place your cursor where you want to add a scrolling text box. Type in something that tells users what you want them to write in the scrolling text box, then press Enter. Click on the scrolling text box button on the Forms toolbar.

6 Save your Web page, and then load it into your browser and even experiment with entering text into it. In the next chapter, you will learn how to let users submit this data so it can be collected.

2 Double-click on the new text box. The Scrolling Text Box Properties dialog box will appear. In the Name field, type in a name for the scrolling text box.

3 If you want text to appear in the scrolling text box (users can replace this text if they choose), then enter this text into the Initial Value field of the dialog box.

4 Enter the Width (in characters) that you want the scrolling text box to be. Enter the Number of lines that you want the scrolling text box to show in the browser window.

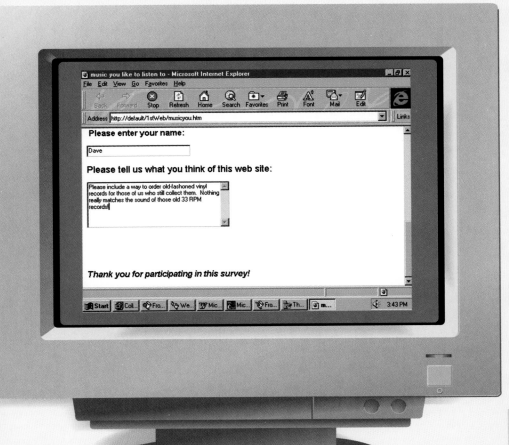

5 Click OK in the Scrolling Text Box Properties dialog box. The scrolling text box will appear on your Web page. If you want to resize it, you can do so by placing your cursor over the edges of the box and dragging the edges to shrink or enlarge the box.

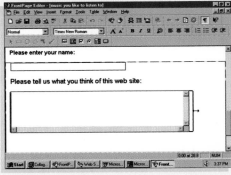

CHAPTER 7

Collecting Data from Your Form

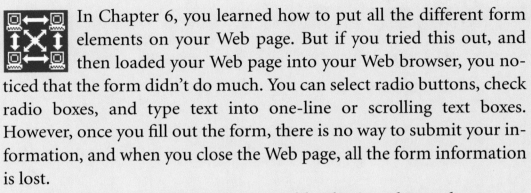In Chapter 6, you learned how to put all the different form elements on your Web page. But if you tried this out, and then loaded your Web page into your Web browser, you noticed that the form didn't do much. You can select radio buttons, check radio boxes, and type text into one-line or scrolling text boxes. However, once you fill out the form, there is no way to submit your information, and when you close the Web page, all the form information is lost.

In this chapter you'll learn how to add Submit and Reset buttons to your Web pages so that users can submit information or reset the form to the default values you specify. You'll also learn how to use the Form Properties dialog box to define where form data gets sent when a user submits your form. In a sense, Chapter 6 and Chapter 7 are like two sides of a coin—you can't use one without the other!

How to Organize Input into Forms

You can have more than one element in a form — most forms have many text fields, check boxes, and radio buttons. On this page you'll get some hints about organizing your forms so that they are easy to use, and so that the data you get back from the forms is easy to interpret.

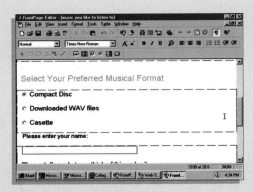

1 In FrontPage Editor, open a Web page which has some form elements added to it.

TIP SHEET

▶ When a user actually submits a form, the file that collects the data lists two things: the form element name and the form element value. For example, the music check boxes that you see on this page get listed in the form output as "Jazz: ON" if it is selected or just "Jazz: " if it is not selected. So make sure that you've given all of your form elements names that you will be able to decipher when you read the form data file.

▶ You can rearrange your form using any of the cut and paste methods that were described in Chapter 3. Using the Cut, Paste, and Copy buttons on the FrontPage Editor toolbar is an especially quick way to edit your form. If you're comfortable with click-and-drag editing, use that.

▶ Although the dotted form outline that you see in the FrontPage Editor window doesn't show up in your Web browser, it's important to keep an eye on it. If you decide you need two separate forms on one Web page, you have to make sure that you have two completely separate dotted form outlines. Otherwise, you'll get all of your form data going to one data file, instead of two.

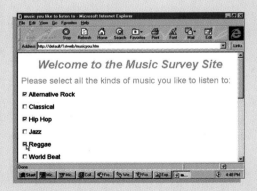

6 Once you've rearranged and redesigned your form to the exact way you want it to look, check it out in your Web browser one last time. If it's perfect, then you're ready to start designing the data collection part of the form. That's what the rest of this chapter is about.

 Make sure that you've entered all of the form fields that you want. You should always put profile fields (such as name and address) at the top of your form. Your form questions should proceed from general questions at the beginning to specific questions at the end. You may also want to reorder the check box or radio button option lists. You can cut and paste form elements just like regular text. Simply highlight the element, choose Cut from the Edit menu, then place your cursor where you want the form element to be, and choose Paste from the Edit menu.

 When you created your first form element, and the form outline was created, you may have ended up with a sentence that introduces a form element being outside of the actual form.

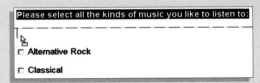

 To fix this, simply place your cursor at the left margin, just before the first form element, and click. FrontPage 97 allows you to use the same click-and-drag text editing feature found in Microsoft Word—just select the text, and with the mouse button pressed down, drag to the new location and release the mouse button.

 If you decide that you want to change some of the attributes of a certain form element, you can do this quite easily. Simply double-click on the check box, radio button, or text box, and the Properties dialog box for that form element will appear.

How to Collect Input with Push Buttons

An online form is no good to you, or to the Web page visitor, unless the data that the user enters can be submitted. It's also handy to allow users to be able to reset all of the form fields to the defaults that you defined when you created each Web element. That way, if users get confused while entering information and they wish to start over, they can do so without having to reload the page. On this page, you'll learn how to create Submit and Reset buttons for your form.

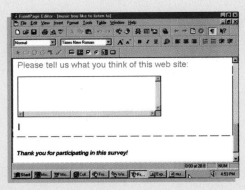

1 Open the Web page that has your form on it in FrontPage Editor. Scroll down to the bottom of your form, and place your cursor inside the form outline at the bottom. (You may have to place your cursor at the end of the last form element and press Enter to get down to a new paragraph.)

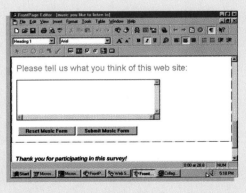

6 The Submit push button will appear in your form. It looks like your form is finished, but you haven't yet defined what happens to the form data when the user clicks the Submit button. On the following pages you'll learn how to set this up.

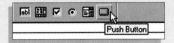

2 Click on the Push Button icon on the Forms toolbar.

3 Double-click on the new push button. The Push Button Properties dialog box will appear. For Button type, select Reset. You can type an appropriate name in the Name field. The Value/Label field defines what the label on the push button will say. The default is Reset, but you can customize this. When you've changed the names, click OK.

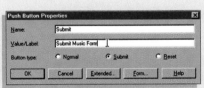

5 Click on the Push Button icon on the toolbar again. This time, leave Submit as the Button type in the Push Button Properties dialog box. You can type in a Name for the Submit button; this is the name you will see in the data file after the form is collected. You can change the Value/Label for the Submit button, this is the label the user will see on the push button. Click OK when you're finished.

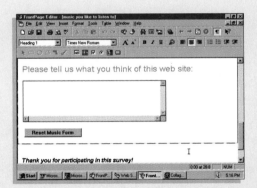

4 The Reset push button will appear on your form, with the label you defined in the dialog box. When users click on this button on your Web page, all the form elements will be set back to their defaults (any selections or text entered by the user will disappear).

How to Save Input to Files

When users press the Submit button on the form in your Web page, the data they've entered is submitted to the Web server where your Web page is located. The Web server takes the data and appends it to a file where all the form data gets stored. On this page you'll learn how to use the automatic form processing bot (short for robot) to specify what file name and type the form output should go to.

▶ **In the Form Properties dialog box, you'll see a section on Hidden Fields. This is an advanced mechanism for having extra information sent to the form output file, without the user knowing about it.**

▶ **The Form Handler pull-down menu lists a number of different automatic form handlers — the Save Results WebBot Component is a fine, generic form handler. The others are for very specific types of forms.**

▶ **The Advanced tab of the Settings for Saving Results of Form dialog box gives you the option of only saving data from certain fields of a form, and also allows the form data to be saved to a second file in addition to the one you specified on the Results tab.**

▶ **The file that all the form data is sent to will be located within your Web site. Switch to FrontPage Explorer, refresh the view and double-click on the file you designated as the results file. If it is a text file, your default text editor will open.**

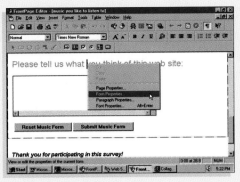

▶ **1** Have your Web page with your form open in FrontPage Editor. Place your cursor anywhere inside the dotted form outline and then click with your right mouse button. From the shortcut menu, choose Form Properties.

9 When you've submitted your form, open the form output file to view the results.

8 You're ready to test out your form. Save your page to your Web site and then load it into your Web page. Make some selections and text entries, and then submit the form. When the Form Confirmation page appears, click on the hyperlink to Return to the Form.

2 In the Form Properties dialog box, select Save Results WebBot Component from the Form Handler pull-down list.

3 After selecting Save Results WebBot Component, click on the Settings button in the Form Properties dialog box.

4 The Settings for Saving Results of Form dialog box will appear. This dialog box has three tabbed layers—Results, Confirm, and Advanced. Only the fields in the Results tab are required to save visitor input. On the Results tab sheet, type a name for the file you want the form information to go to in the File for results field.

5 You must choose what file format you want the form results to be saved to. If you want the form results to become another Web page, choose HTML for the file format. You can also send the output to go to a formatted text file. To do that, choose the type of file you want from the File Format pull-down menu. Then make sure that the Include field names in output check box is selected.

7 The Confirm tab allows you to define a Confirmation page. If you want a confirmation page to appear, specify the file name of your confirmation Web page in the URL of Confirmation page field. The Advanced tab allows you to define a second results file. These components are optional. After you have completed the Settings for Saving Results of Form dialog box, click OK. Click OK in the Form Properties dialog box to save your settings.

6 You can also choose to have the date and time and other data appended to the form data. Choose these options from the Additional Information to Save section of the dialog box.

TRY IT!

Once again it is time to put into practice the concepts you've learned in the past few chapters. You can continue to enhance the Web page for the Little Theater's production of Romeo and Juliet. Now the Little Theater wants you to create a form which will allow users to request a brochure and ticket order form for the production.

Open the Web page you created in the previous Try It! section.

In FrontPage Editor, scroll down to the bottom of the Web page and place your cursor in a new paragraph.

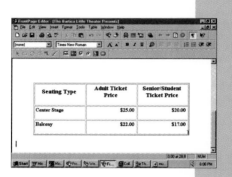

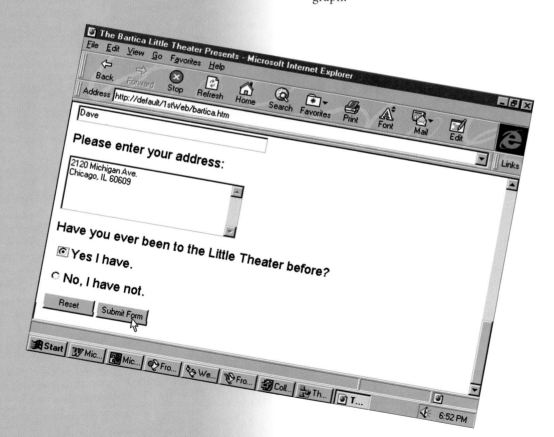

3

Type in a sentence to introduce the brochure request form.

4

Type in a sentence to indicate that users should enter their names. Then click on the one-line text box button on the Forms toolbar.

5

Double-click on the new text box. In the Text Box Properties dialog box, type CustomerName into the Name field. Then increase the text box width from 20 characters to 50 characters. Click OK.

6

Place your cursor after the text box and then press Enter to get to a new paragraph. Type in a sentence telling users to enter their address. Then press Enter again.

7

Click on the scrolling text button on the toolbar. Double-click in the new text box.

8

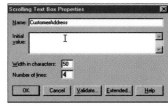

In the Scrolling Text Properties dialog box, type CustomerAddress in the name field. Change the width in characters to 50, and change the number of lines to 4. Then click OK.

9

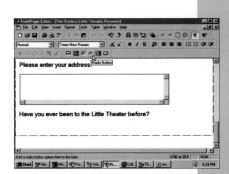

With your cursor after the scrolling text box, press Enter. Type a sentence asking users whether they've ever been to the Little Theater before. Press Enter and then click on the radio button icon on the Forms toolbar.

10

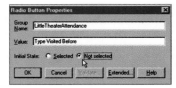

Double-click on the radio button. In the Radio Button Properties dialog box, type LittleTheaterAttendance as the Group Name. Type Visited Before as the Value and set the initial state as Not Selected. Click OK.

Continue to next page ▶

TRY IT!

Continue below

11

Type a sentence beside the radio button, such as "Yes, I have." Press Enter.

12

Click on the radio button icon on the Forms toolbar again. Double-click on the new radio button and enter LittleTheaterAttendance again for the Group Name. Type in Never Visited Before as the Value. Define the initial state as Not Selected and click OK.

13

Type a sentence beside the radio button, such as "No, I have not." Press Enter. Click on the push button icon on the toolbar.

14

Double-click on the new push button. In the Push Button Properties dialog box, select Reset as the Button type. Type Reset in as the Name, then click OK.

15

Click on the push button icon on the toolbar again. Double-click on the new button. This time select Submit as the Button type in the Push Button Properties dialog box. Enter SubmitForm for the Name field. Type Submit Form for the Value/Label field, then click OK.

16

Now right-click your mouse button with your cursor inside the form outline. From the shortcut menu, select Form Properties.

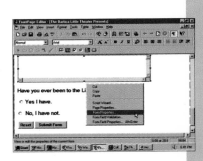

17

In the Form Properties dialog box, select the Save Results WebBot Component from the Form Handler pull-down menu. Then click on the Settings button.

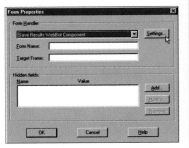

18

In the Settings for Saving Results of Form dialog box, type a name for the file which will store all the form re-sults. Make sure the Include field names in output check box is selected. Select Formatted text as the File Format. Select the Time and Date check boxes in the Additional information to save section. Then click OK.

19

Click OK in the Form Properties di-alog box to save the form settings. Then save the Web page by clicking on the save but-ton on the toolbar.

20

Click the Preview in Browser but-ton so that you can check out your Web page. You may have to press reload to see your recent additions.

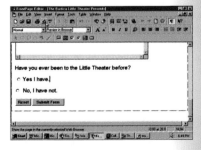

21

Scroll down to the form, and fill it out. Then press the submit button.

22

You should get a Security alert — just click Yes. Then you'll see the auto-matically generated Confirmation page, with a link back to the Form.

23

Open the form output file by double-clicking on it in FrontPage Explorer.

24

When the file opens, you should see the data you entered into the form listed.
Congratulations! You now have a working form that collects customer information!

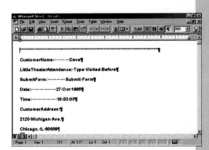

CHAPTER 8

Using Bookmarks to Create Links in Your Web Page

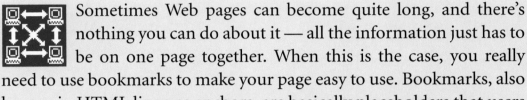 Sometimes Web pages can become quite long, and there's nothing you can do about it — all the information just has to be on one page together. When this is the case, you really need to use bookmarks to make your page easy to use. Bookmarks, also known in HTML lingo as anchors, are basically placeholders that users can get to easily. For instance, you may want users to be able to get back to the top of a Web page with a simple mouse click. By putting a bookmark at the top of a Web page, and a link to that bookmark after every section of your page, users will be able to get back to the top of the page with ease.

This chapter will show you how to create a bookmark, how to create a link to a bookmark, and how to create a table of contents using bookmarks.

How to Assign Link Properties to Bookmarks

You can define bookmarks anywhere on a Web page. And you can have as many bookmarks as you like on any single page. Then you can refer to these bookmarks from anywhere on the same page, or from any other Web page for that matter. But in this section, you'll learn specifically how to create the bookmark itself.

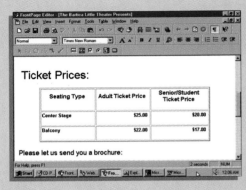

 1 In FrontPage Editor, open one of your Web pages that already has some content on it.

▶ **You can only create a bookmark on text elements of your Web page. You can't make a bookmark out of a picture or on a blank line.**

▶ **It's generally a good idea to try to give all of the bookmarks on the same Web page very distinct names. This will help later on when you go to create a link to a bookmark, and you have to pick the bookmark you want from a list of all the bookmarks on that page.**

5 You can create as many bookmarks as you think you need. Your Web page won't look much different when you're done, except that anything that is a bookmark will have a dotted blue line underneath it. These lines won't show up in your Web browser. On the following pages, you'll see how to create links to these new bookmarks.

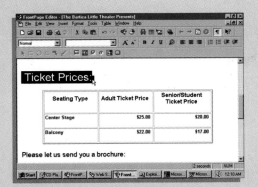

2 Highlight the text that you want made into a bookmark. This is the part of the page that will be shown when people click on a link to this bookmark.

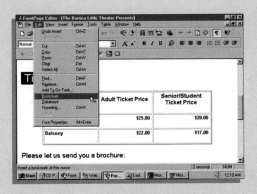

3 From the Edit menu, select Bookmark.

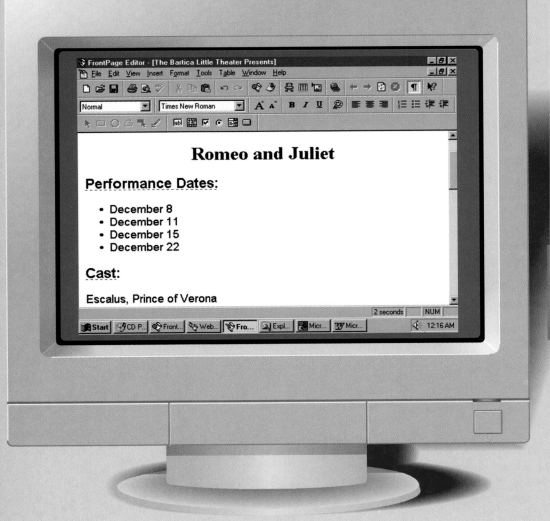

4 In the Bookmark dialog box, the text you selected will automatically show up as the bookmark name. You can leave this as it is, or you can type in a name that is shorter and easier to remember. Click OK when you are finished.

How to Create Links to Bookmarks from Text

N ow that you've created a few bookmarks on your Web page, you're probably ready to create some links to those bookmarks. If you've got them, you might as well use them, right?

Follow the steps on this page to create as many bookmark links as you need. When you're finished, users will see blue, highlighted, underlined text when they view your page with their Web browser. And when they can click on the bookmark links, different parts of your Web page will be displayed for them.

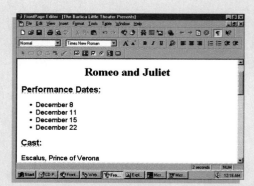

1 In FrontPage Editor, open a Web page on which you've created some bookmarks.

6 You'll now see that the sentence you originally typed in is blue and underlined. You can use Ctrl+Click to follow the link without leaving the FrontPage Editor.

TIP SHEET

▶ When you test your site with your browser, you'll probably notice that the bookmark links aren't blue, they're some other color. This is because the links are to the current page, which browsers consider to be a "visited link." Therefore, these links will not be the regular blue color of unvisited links. Of course, if you've set up your browser so that the different types of links have custom colors, then you may have no blue links at all!

▶ You don't necessarily need a whole sentence to tell users where a bookmark link will take them. Often a simple "TOP" or "PAGE BOTTOM" link will do. Whatever you decide to use as your bookmark link phrases, make sure that you are consistent across all of the Web pages in your Web site.

▶ When the user places a cursor over the top of the bookmark link in their browser, the bookmark link is shown in the bottom status bar of the browser, complete with the number sign.

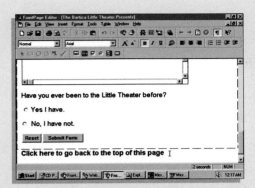

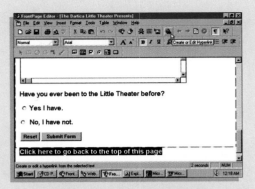

2 Decide where you want to create a link to a bookmark. For example, at the end of a certain section you may want to create a link to the top of the Web page. Place your cursor in this area. Type in a sentence, such as "Click here to go back to the top of this page."

3 Highlight your sentence and then click on the Create or Edit Hyperlinks button on the toolbar.

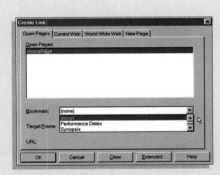

4 The Create Hyperlink dialog box will appear. Make sure that the Open Pages tab is on top. In the Bookmark field, click on the down arrow of the pull-down menu to view all of the bookmarks that are on the current Web page.

5 Select a bookmark that you created near the top of the Web page. Notice that "bookmark URL:" appears at the bottom of the dialog box. The number sign means that the URL (Internet address) for the link being created is a bookmark. Click OK.

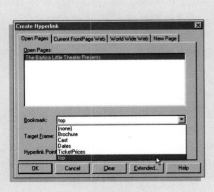

How to Use Bookmarks to Create a Table of Contents

Bookmarks can be quite useful for creating a Table of Contents for your Web page. When you have a lot of information on your Web page that is separated into distinct sections, you'll want people who visit your page to be able to get to each section quickly, without having to search through your page. Creating a Table of Contents allows your visitors to get to the information they want with a single mouse click.

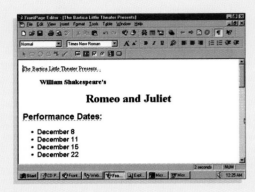

1 In FrontPage Editor, open up a Web page that has a large amount of content on it.

TIP SHEET

▶ There are a number of other ways to go about making a Table of Contents in Microsoft FrontPage. There is a template that helps you to construct a Table of Contents for a whole Web site, and there is a robot that automatically generates a Table of Contents from your Web page's headings. Both of these topics will be covered in later chapters. For now, the method on this page is a way to create a simple table of contents for your visitors.

▶ If you only have two sections on your Web page, a Table of Contents may be overdoing it. You may just want to create a single bookmark link that says something like "To view information on XXX, click here."

6 Save your page and load it into your Web browser to see how your new Table of Contents works.

Follow the instructions from earlier in this chapter to create bookmarks for each section of your Web page.

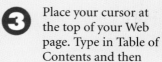 Place your cursor at the top of your Web page. Type in Table of Contents and then press Enter.

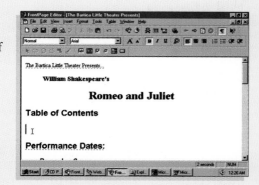

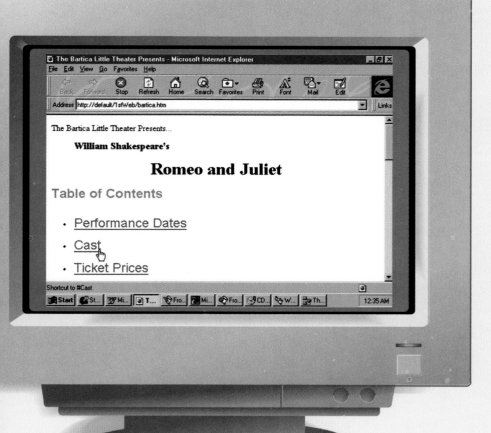

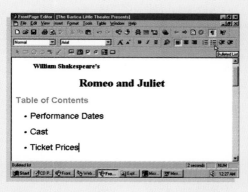

Type in the names of each of the different sections of your Web page. Then highlight all of these section names and click on the bulleted list icon on the Formatting toolbar.

For each section name that you've typed in, highlight it and click on the Create or Edit Hyperlink button on the toolbar. From the pull-down Bookmark list, select the appropriate bookmark for the section name you've highlighted.

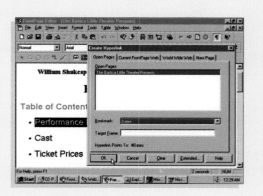

CHAPTER 9

Linking Multiple Pages in Your Web Site

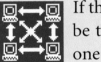 If there weren't any links on the World Wide Web, it wouldn't be the World Wide Web. The hyperlinks that lead you from one page to another are what make the World Wide Web such a dynamic resource. Creating the hyperlinks that allow users to jump from one Web page to another is fairly easy in Microsoft FrontPage.

In this chapter you'll learn how to create links within the Web sites you've already created. With these links visitors will be able to go back and forth between your various Web pages. In the next chapter you'll learn how to create links to Web pages on Internet servers around the world.

How to Link Your Web Page to Other Pages in Your Web Site

Within most Web sites you will find links that will lead you back to a central page in the site, or to a few of the main pages within the site. For instance, most universities have Web sites, and on almost every page within the Web site there will be a few links: "Click here to go to the University Home Page," "Click here to go to the Faculty Listing," and "Click here to go to the Academic Calendar." The consistency of such links is what makes the Web site, as a whole, easy to navigate.

On this page you'll learn how to create links that allow users to jump from one page in your Web site to another page in your Web site.

TIP SHEET

▶ In the Create Hyperlink dialog box, you may have noticed the Target Frame field. If you are creating the link in a Web page that has a number of separate frames, you can indicate that when users select this link, then the page that is being linked to should be opened in one of the frames already showing in the browser window. You will learn more about this in Chapter 15, "Framing Your Pages."

▶ You can have as many links as you like on your Web page, and within all of the pages in your Web site. The important thing is to make sure that you are consistent with your links.

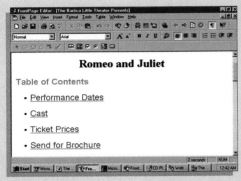

▶ **1** Open a Web page in FrontPage Editor.

8 Save your Web page, and load it into your Web browser. Then click on your new link to see how it works.

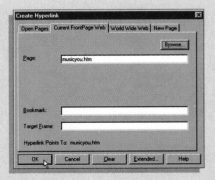

7 In the Create Hyperlink dialog box, the page you selected should be listed in the Page field. If you wish to link to a specific part of that Web page using a bookmark you've created for that page already, you can choose the bookmark from the Bookmark pull-down menu. If there aren't any bookmarks created for the page you've selected, there won't be a pull-down menu in the Bookmark field. Click OK to create your

2 Place your cursor at the bottom of the page, and type in a sentence indicating that users can click to get to a different page within your Web site.

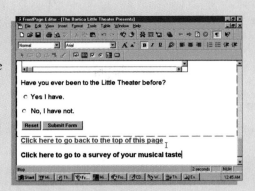

3 Highlight part or all of your sentence and then click on the Create or Edit Hyperlinks button on the toolbar.

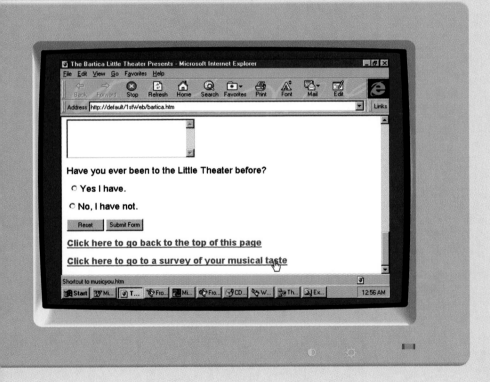

4 In the Create Hyperlink dialog box, click on the Current FrontPage Web tab.

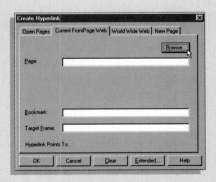

5 On the Current FrontPage Web tab, click on the Browse button.

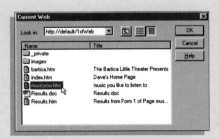

6 In the Current Web dialog box, select the Web page you wish to create a link to, and then click OK.

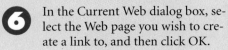

How to Link Pages in Separate Webs

Many people who create Web sites will create more than one individual site. For example, you may create a home page for yourself and your family, and then you may create a separate Web site for your business. Each of the two Web sites could have four or five different Web pages, and they could be stored on the same computer. The difference is that one Web site is stored in one directory and the other Web site is stored in a different directory.

To create a link from a page in one Web site to a page that is in another of your Web sites, follow the steps on this page.

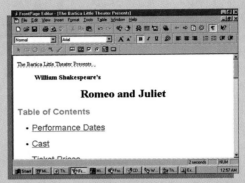

1 In FrontPage Editor, open the Web page on which you wish to create a link.

TIP SHEET

▶ **If you are creating a link to a Web site that you have created and stored on an Internet server somewhere, then you will have to enter the Internet server name (www.servername.com) in the URL field, in place of localhost.**

▶ **If you can't remember the Web site name, or the Web page name that you are trying to link to, this is not a problem. Simply switch to FrontPage Explorer, and load the Web site. All the localhost Web site names will be listed in the Open Web dialog box. Once you load up the Web site, you just have to highlight the Web page in the Outline view. Then right-click and choose Properties to find out the file name of the Web page. Make sure you reload your original Web site before switching back to FrontPage Editor!**

6 Now save your page, and load it into your browser. Click on your new link to make sure it works.

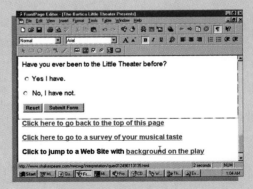

5 The linked part of your sentence will be blue and underlined in FrontPage Editor. The linked URL displays in the Status Bar.

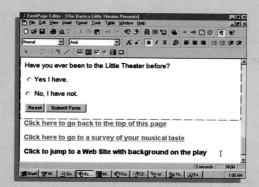

2 Place your cursor wherever you'd like to put a link to your other Web site. Type in a sentence for the link.

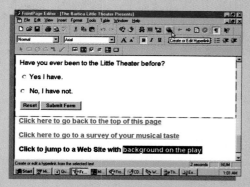

3 Highlight the part of the sentence you want linked and click on the Create or Edit Hyperlink button on the toolbar.

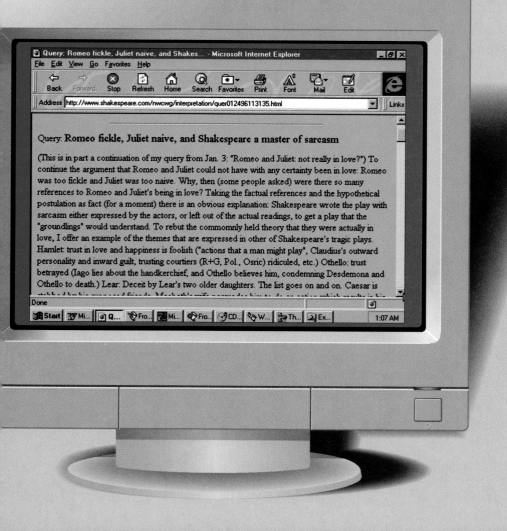

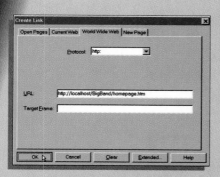

4 Select the World Wide Web tab of the Create Hyperlink dialog box. Make sure that the protocol field is set to http://. Then, in the URL field, place your cursor after http://, and type the URL of the site that you wish to link to. Click OK when you are finished.

How to Link to a New Page in Your Web

Sometimes when you're creating a Web page, you will want to create a link to a Web page that doesn't yet exist. You know that you're going to create a certain Web page soon, and you want to create a link for it on the page you are currently working on. Of course, a page that doesn't yet exist won't be listed in the Current Web dialog box. But, FrontPage Editor has a way around this little snag, as you'll see on this page.

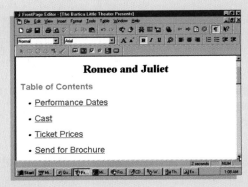

1 In FrontPage Editor, open the Web page on which you wish to create a link.

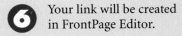

6 Your link will be created in FrontPage Editor.

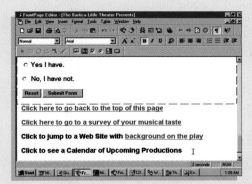

2 Place your cursor wherever you'd like to put a link to your other Web site. Type in a sentence for the link.

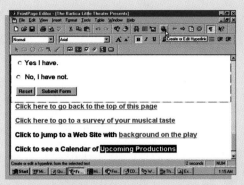

3 Highlight the part of the sentence that you want linked and click on the Create or Edit Hyperlink button on the toolbar.

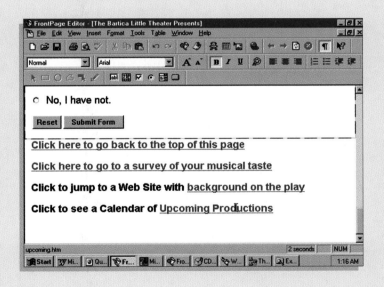

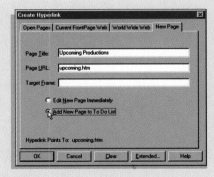

4 Select the New Page tab of the Create Link dialog box. You must enter a title and a file name for your new page. At this point you have to make a choice about whether you want to edit the new page right now, or whether you want to put it on to your to do list. You should probably put it on to your to do list, and continue working with your current page. Click OK.

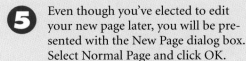

5 Even though you've elected to edit your new page later, you will be presented with the New Page dialog box. Select Normal Page and click OK.

CHAPTER 10

Linking Your Web Site to the World Wide Web

In the previous chapter you learned how to hyperlink your Web pages together. And you learned how to create hyperlinks from Web pages in one of your Internet sites to another one of your Internet sites. However, the Internet sites that you create with Microsoft FrontPage are not the only Internet sites around. As you well know, the World Wide Web is populated with millions of different home pages and Web sites.

In this chapter you'll learn how to create hyperlinks to other Web pages that are located on remote Internet servers. After all, your Web page wouldn't be much of a Web page if it didn't contain some Internet hyperlinks! There is so much information available on the Web, and by adding hyperlinks to information that is relevant to your Web site, you're providing a great service to your visitors.

How to Create Hyperlinks to Other WWW Sites

Hyperlinks to pages on the World Wide Web always use the HTTP protocol. HTTP stands for HyperText Transfer Protocol, and it is this computer protocol that allows Web pages to be transferred from Internet servers to your desktop computer. On this page you'll learn a little bit about the structure of a World Wide Web address, which always begins with "http://."

To create a hyperlink on your Web page to another Web page that is located somewhere on the Internet, follow the steps on this page.

TIP SHEET

▶ **If you don't know the Internet address of the Web page you are trying to create a hyperlink to, don't worry. All you have to do is use the Browse button in the World Wide Web tab of the Create Hyperlink dialog box to search for the site to which you want to link.**

▶ **The other hyperlink types that you see if you click on the pull-down menu of the Protocol field are used for connecting to Internet resources other than Web pages. For example, there is "ftp://" for connecting to a File Transfer Protocol site and there is "mailto:" which you will use later in this chapter for creating e-mail hyperlinks.**

▶ **If your hyperlink doesn't work when you test it in your browser, make sure that you have typed in the exact URL of the Web page you are trying to connect to. Web page addresses can be quite tricky and they are case-sensitive, so make sure you've capitalized letters that are supposed to be capitalized.**

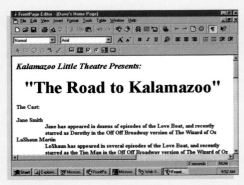

1 In FrontPage Editor, open up a Web page that you'd like to add some Internet hyperlinks to.

6 Your hyperlink will now be blue and underlined in FrontPage Editor. Save your Web page and load it into your browser so that you can see if your hyperlink works. Make sure you get online first, though!

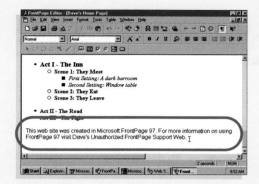

 Type in a sentence or a name for the Web page that you are creating the hyperlink to.

3 Highlight part or all of the sentence you just typed in and then click on the Create or Edit Hyperlink button on the toolbar.

4 In the Create Hyperlink dialog box, select the World Wide Web tab.

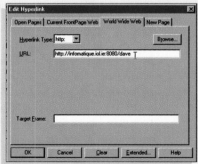

5 Make sure that the Hyperlink type field is set to "http://." Place your cursor in the URL field, after "http://." Type in the rest of the Web page address for the Web page you wish to create a hyperlink to. The Web page address should look something like this: http://www.servername.com/ DirectoryStructure/WebPageName .html. Then click OK.

How to Refine Hyperlinks to Other Sites

Sometimes you may need to get rid of one of the hyperlinks on your Web page, or you may need to change a hyperlink, because the page that hyperlink is supposed to point to has a new URL. Both of these tasks are easy to accomplish in FrontPage Editor. Just follow the steps on this page, and your hyperlinks will all be perfect again!

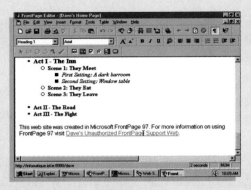

▶ **1** In FrontPage Editor, open the page which has the hyperlink you'd like to change or delete.

▶ **Web page URLs tend to change a lot. It can take a lot of effort just to make sure that all of the hyperlinks you have in your Web site are current and correct. But Microsoft FrontPage Explorer has a few features to help save you some time and trouble. You won't have to go visit each hyperlink destination yourself just to make sure the hyperlinks are still valid. In Chapter 17 you will see how FrontPage Explorer does all of this dirty work for you. However, if you want to make sure that the content of the Web pages you are linking to is still valid, then you'll have to check this for yourself. FrontPage only checks to see if the page still exists.**

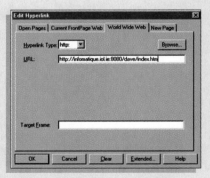

5 The Edit Hyperlink dialog box will open up, with the World Wide Web tab on top. Enter the changed URL in the URL field. Then click OK.

2 If you want to delete a hyperlink, and you want to delete the whole sentence that points to the hyperlink as well, all you have to do is select the sentence (hyperlink and all) and hit the delete key or choose Clear from the Edit menu.

3 If you would like to get rid of a hyperlink, but leave behind the text that was hyperlinked, select the hyperlink. Then, from the Edit menu, choose Unlink.

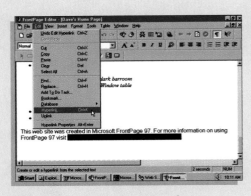

4 If the URL of one your hyperlinks has changed, highlight the hyperlink. Then, from the Edit menu choose Hyperlink.

How to Create E-Mail Hyperlinks

Although the Internet has a number of different parts, the World Wide Web and e-mail are definitely the two fastest growing parts of the Internet. Every day, more and more people are getting Internet accounts so that they can have access to Internet e-mail and to surf the World Wide Web. Most browsers in use now have the ability to allow users to send e-mail from a Web page. So you can include an e-mail hyperlink from on your Web page, and people who don't even have e-mail addresses will be able to send you e-mail (provided that you have an e-mail account!). As long as someone can load your Web page into their browser, they can send you e-mail.

On this page you'll learn how to add an e-mail hyperlink to your Web page, and you'll see what happens when somebody clicks on your e-mail hyperlink.

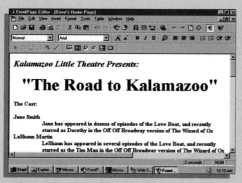

1 Open your Web page in FrontPage Editor.

TIP SHEET

▶ When you receive e-mail that has originated from your Web page, you will be able to tell that it is from your Web page. The e-mail will have the return address that is associated with the user's Internet account. So if someone is sitting in a cybercafe somewhere, and sends you e-mail, you'll get the return address of the cybercafe, but not of the individual who sent the mail.

▶ You can create an e-mail hyperlink with anybody's e-mail address, it doesn't have to be the address of the person who created the home page. However, that is usually the appropriate address to include on a Web page.

6 You should see a typical e-mail screen like the one shown here. Send yourself an e-mail to make sure that your hyperlink works!

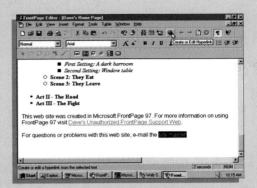

2 Type in a sentence for your e-mail hyperlink. Then highlight it and select the Create or Edit Hyperlink button from the toolbar.

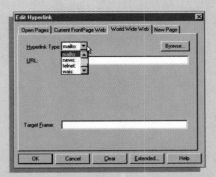

3 In the Edit Hyperlink dialog box, select the World Wide Web tab. In the Hyperlink Type field, click on the down arrow to view the pull-down list.

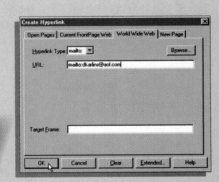

4 Scroll through the Hyperlink Type list and select "mailto:". Then in the URL field below, enter your e-mail address after "mailto:" and click OK.

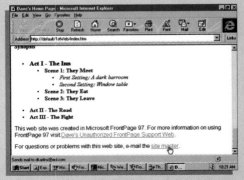

5 You now have an e-mail hyperlink on your Web page. Save your page and load it into your browser. Then click on the e-mail hyperlink.

TRY IT!

Once again, it is time to put your newly acquired FrontPage skills to the test. Your local Little Theater wants you to create a Table of Contents for the Romeo and Juliet page. The Little Theater wants you to create a new page for them, containing information about other upcoming shows and season ticket information. They don't want this page created right this instant, but you figure that you might as well create a link to it from the Romeo and Juliet page now, while you're working on it. They also want a link to the home page of the Little Theater Association.

Open the Romeo and Juliet page in FrontPage Editor.

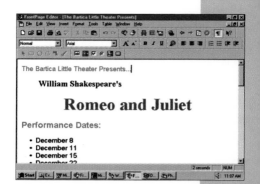

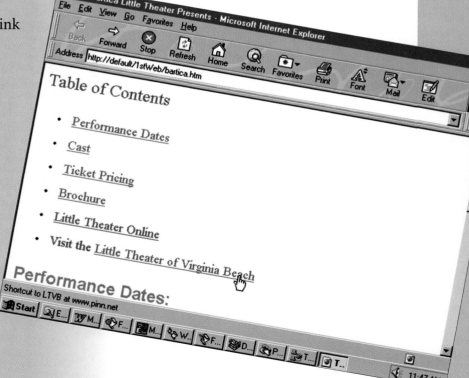

First you'll want to create a Table of Contents. Highlight "Performance Dates" and then select Bookmark from the Edit menu.

In the Bookmark dialog box, the words you highlighted will be the default Bookmark Name. Click OK.

Repeat this for each of the sections on the Romeo and Juliet page.

At the top of the page, type in Table of Contents. Then press Enter.

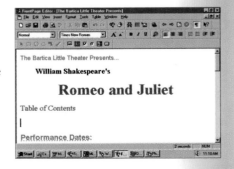

Type in the name of each section on your page, pressing Enter after each section name.

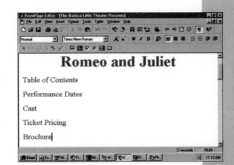

Highlight this list and format it as a bulleted list.

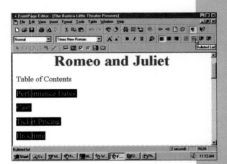

Highlight the first section name. Select the Create or Edit Hyperlink button from the toolbar.

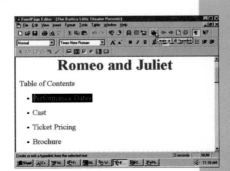

Continue to next page ▶

TRY IT!

Continue below

In the Create Link dialog box, select the Open Pages tab. Then click on

the down arrow of the Bookmark field to view the list of bookmarks on this page. Select the appropriate bookmark and click OK.

Repeat steps 8 and 9 for all of the section names in your Table of Contents.

Now that you've created a Table of Contents, you want to create a link to a new Web page for the Little Theater. The new Web page will give information about upcoming shows, auditions, and season ticket information. It will be called Bartica Little Theater Online. Type in a sentence for a link to this Web page on the Romeo and Juliet page.

Highlight the part of the sentence you want as the link, and then click on the Create or Edit

Hyperlinks button on the toolbar.

In the Create Hyperlink dialog box, select the New Page tab. The words you selected for the link will be the default

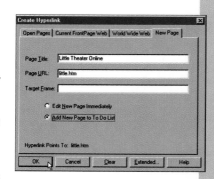

title for the new page. You can leave this as it is or change it. Type in a file-name (URL) for the new page. Little would be a good name — you don't have to add the .htm, it is added automatically. You'll want to come back later to create the content for this new page, so select "Add New Page to To Do List." Click OK when you're done.

The New Page dialog box will appear. Select Normal Page and click OK.

Okay the Save As dialog box to save the new page in your FrontPage Web.

Add a link to the Little Theater of Virginia Beach home page. The URL is http://www.pinn.net/LTVB/. Type in a sentence for this link on the Romeo and Juliet page.

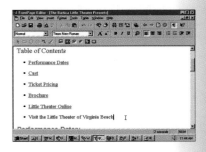

Highlight the part of the sentence you want as the link, and click on the Create or Edit Hyperlink button on the toolbar.

In the Create Hyperlink dialog box, select the World Wide Web tab. In the Protocol field, make sure that "http://" is selected. In the URL field, place your cursor after http:// and type in www.pinn.net/LTVB. Then click OK.

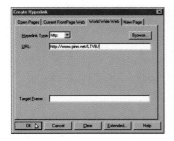

Save your Web page.

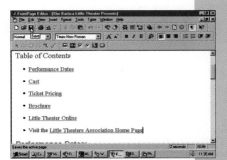

Preview the Romeo and Juliet page with your Web browser to see all the new additions to your Web page!

CHAPTER 11

Using the FrontPage Templates

By this time, you are well aware of how quick and easy it is to create Web pages using Microsoft FrontPage. What you are about to find out is that it can be even quicker and easier to create Web pages with Microsoft FrontPage. That's because FrontPage comes with a number of pre-built Web pages that you can use for a variety of purposes. All you have to do is enter the appropriate information, and the FrontPage templates take care of the spacing, formatting, linking, and layout of your page. Some of the templates even use Wizards that can lead you through the design of your Web page, step by step.

In this chapter you will learn how to use the FrontPage templates, and you'll see examples of a few of the most useful templates, including the Guest Book and the Personal Home Page Wizard.

How to Use the Templates

On this page you'll find out how to access the templates, and what's involved in using them. Using a template is much like filling in a form—the layout and setup for the information is already there; all you have to do is add the content. With many of the Web page templates, you'll also find that hyperlinks, bookmarks, forms, and tables have already been created for you. In many cases, the only work left for you to do is to highlight the default text and replace it with your own customized text.

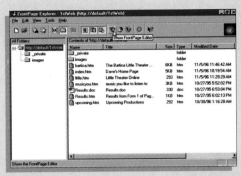

▶ **1** Open your Web in FrontPage Explorer. Then switch to FrontPage Editor by clicking on the Show FrontPage Editor button on the toolbar.

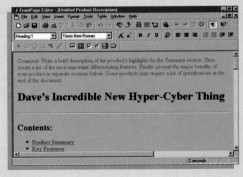

7 All you really have to do on this Web page is select the text that is already there, and replace it with your own. For example, in the Product Summary section of the template, there is a suggestion for you to include a picture and a brief introduction of the product. All you have to do is follow the suggestions. (You'll learn how to add images to your page in the next chapter.) When you're finished adding your own content, save your new Web page.

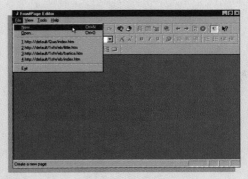

2 In FrontPage Editor, choose New from the File menu.

3 In the New Page dialog box, scroll through the templates to get a good idea of the variety that are available to you. There are lots of business-oriented templates, and a number of templates for educational purposes as well.

4 If you select a template name, you can read a description of that template at the bottom of the dialog box. To see how the template works, select the Product Description template, and click OK.

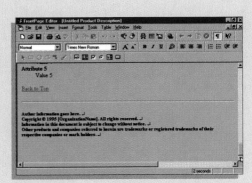

6 If you scroll through the Web page you will notice that there is already a Table of Contents set up, with bookmarks and hyperlinks from each section to the top of the page. At the bottom of the Web page you will see a default copyright paragraph.

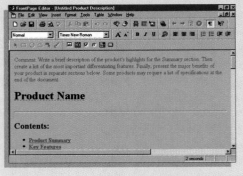

5 In FrontPage Editor, a Product Description Web page will appear. The purple writing at the top of the page contains instructions for using the template. You don't have to delete these instructions, they won't show up in anyone's Web browser.

How to Create a Guest Book

You've probably come across numerous guest books if you've been surfing the World Wide Web for a while. Guest books are a great way to create a personal hyperlink between the Web site visitors and the Web site authors. Most Web site authors don't get the chance to meet the people who visit their sites, nor do they get to find out what their visitors think of their sites. With a guest book, a Web site visitor can leave a message identifying themselves and telling the Web site author what they think.

 1 In FrontPage Editor, select New from the File menu. In the New Page dialog box, select Guest Book and click OK.

TIP SHEET

▶ **You can change the output file name, or even the output format, of the Guest Book by editing the form properties on the Guest Book page. The default is for the Guest Book entries to appear on a Web page. If you leave this as the default, you'll probably want to create a hyperlink to this output page, so that visitors can see who else has visited and what they have said about the site.**

▶ **You'll probably want to load the form output page into FrontPage Editor and edit it. You should give it a title, such as "What people are saying about the Kalamazoo Little Theater Site" and you should add in a hyperlink back to the Web site's home page.**

 7 Now type the form output URL (Guestlog.htm) into your Web browser to see the results of your form entry.

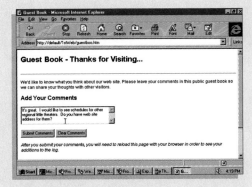

 6 Save your Web page and load it into your Web browser. Click on the hyperlink to the Guest Book. Enter a comment into the Guest Book, and click on the Submit button.

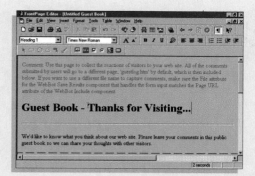

2 The Guest Book template page will appear in FrontPage Editor. Notice that a form area has already been created. You can customize the text that introduces the form by typing in the name of your Web site, or you can just leave it as it is.

3 Choose Save As from the File menu. In the Save As dialog box, accept the defaults or type in another title and file name for the Guest Book. Click OK.

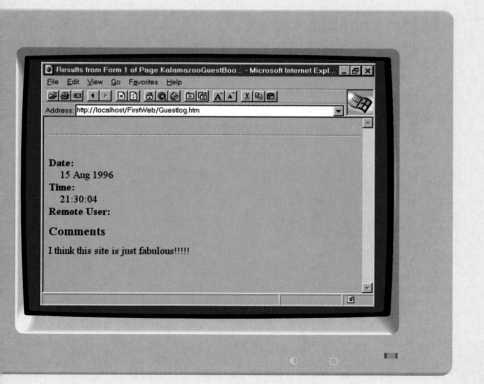

4 If you right-click in the blank area at the bottom of the Web page, you will see a hyperlink to "guestlog.htm." This bot indicates where the results from the form will appear. At the very bottom of the Web page, replace author information, organization name, and so forth with your own customized data.

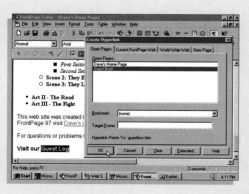

5 In the main Web page of your Web site, type in a sentence for the Guest Book hyperlink. Follow the steps from Chapter 9 to create a hyperlink to your Guest Book page.

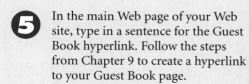

How to Create an Employment Opportunities Page

Another template that is available in Microsoft FrontPage is the Employment Opportunities template. Job information pages are quite common pages for most corporate Web sites, so this template will be useful for anyone creating a company Web site. Just follow the bot instructions and you'll have a job opportunities page for your company so fast they'll want to give you a raise!

1 In FrontPage Editor, select New from the File menu. In the New Page dialog box, select Employment Opportunities and click OK.

6 When you've finished customizing this template, save the Web page. Then, make sure you add a hyperlink for this Web page to the company's home page.

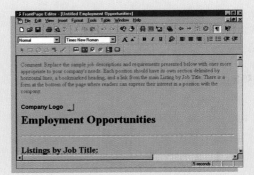

2 The Employment Opportunities template is much like the Product Specification template seen earlier in this chapter — you just have to replace and customize the text.

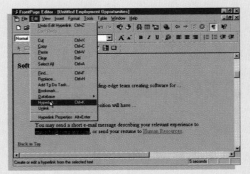

3 There is one new aspect to this template, however, and that is that e-mail hyperlinks have been included. You will see this if you scroll down to the Software Engineering position. Of course the e-mail address that is included is a fake, and you'll need to edit this hyperlink to include a real e-mail address. To do this, select the hyperlink and choose Hyperlink from the Edit menu. Then, edit the e-mail address in the Create Hyperlink dialog box.

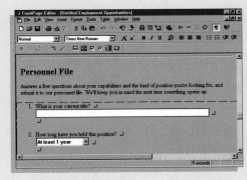

4 At the bottom of this template there is a form that allows Web page visitors to enter their qualifications for your Human Resource Department to keep on file.

5 To find out where the results of this form go, right-click inside the form and choose Form Properties from the pop-up menu. Click on the Settings button in the Form Properties dialog box. You will probably want to edit the settings so that the results of this form get sent to a text file, rather than an HTML page. When you're finished with the settings, click OK and then click OK in the Form Properties dialog box.

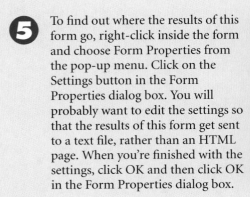

How to Use the Personal Home Page Wizard

Using the Microsoft FrontPage templates to create Web pages is easy. But using the FrontPage Wizard to create Web pages makes using the templates look difficult. That's because the Wizards take care of everything for you. Wizards work by asking you questions. You just answer each question in turn, and at the end of the questions, the Wizard creates your Web page for you. On this page you'll be introduced to the Personal Home Page Wizard. You won't see every single step involved in using the Wizard because that would take a number of pages, but using the Wizard is so simple that the introduction on this page is all you really need.

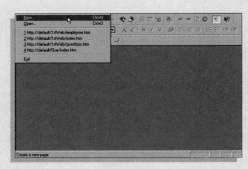

▶ **1** Open FrontPage Editor and choose New from the File menu.

8 When the Wizard is finished, you'll be told to click on the Finish button to generate your Web page. Your new Web page will appear in FrontPage Editor. It's not completely finished — you'll probably need to enter some text. But you're definitely on your way! Enjoy!

7 If you specified a Contact Information section, then you'll have to decide what type of contact information you want to include. If you specified a Comments and Suggestions section, you'll have to tell the Wizard where visitors' comments should go.

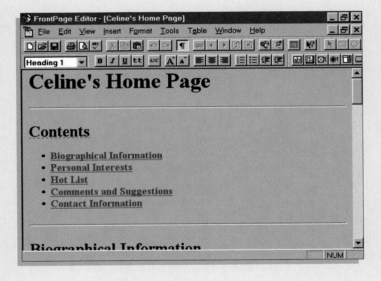

2 In the New Page dialog box, select the Personal Home Page Wizard and click OK.

3 The Personal Home Page Wizard dialog box will appear. Notice that there is a status bar at the bottom of this dialog box. This tells you how far along you are in the process of creating your Web page. There are also Back and Next buttons that allow you to navigate between the Wizard's steps (so that you can go back and change your mind). This first Wizard step asks you to select the sections of information you want on your home page. Make your choices by toggling the check boxes and then click Next.

4 Now the Wizard will ask you what you want to call your Web page and what file name you wish to give it. Customize the names and then click Next.

5 The Wizard steps that appear after this will depend on the choices that you made in the very first Wizard dialog box. You may be asked to specify a format for your Hot List and you may have to select either the Academic, Professional, or Personal style for your biography section.

6 If you included a Personal Interests section, you'll be asked to type in some items for this section.

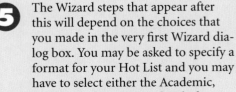

CHAPTER 12

Adding Images to Your Web Page

 The Web pages you've created so far have gained a lot in the way of content. You've learned how to add lists and tables, forms, and hyperlinks. However, you may find that your Web pages are somewhat dull looking, and that they don't compare to the ones you see out on the World Wide Web. What you're probably missing are the graphics and the color that are the hallmark of great Web pages. In the next few chapters you'll learn how to add graphics, graphical hyperlinks, and color to your Web page.

The FrontPage 97 bonus pack includes a free copy of Microsoft Image Composer. Good deal! This chapter in particular will focus on bringing images from Image Composer's selection of clip art into your Web page, and on editing the images on your Web pages. If you want to create your own images in Image Composer, experiment with the program. If you want to get serious about creating graphics in Image Composer, there are books dedicated to that program.

There are two ways to go about adding a picture to your Web page: one is by copying and pasting it in, and the other is to import the image into your Web site. You'll see both of these techniques on the next few pages.

How to Copy Graphics Objects onto Your Page

If you're going to be adding any images to your Web page, you'll need to get yourself a good image editing package. Microsoft Image Composer is a perfect package that is available free in the FrontPage 97 bonus pack.

On this page you'll get a glimpse of how to use Image Composer to find an image.

1 Launch Microsoft Image Composer by clicking on the Show Image Editor button on the FrontPage Explorer toolbar.

7 Your image should appear in the middle of your Web page. If you have too much space below it, move your cursor down to the next paragraph, and delete any extra blank lines you don't want.

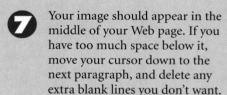

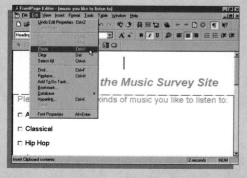

6 If you want your image to be in the middle of your Web page, click on the centering button on the FrontPage Editor toolbar. Now, select Paste from the Edit menu.

TIP SHEET

▶ **In addition to selecting from the graphics already available to you on your the FrontPage CD, you can use Image Composer to create your own images. That is a topic beyond the scope of this book. But don't be afraid to try it— Image Composer is a fun program to play with.**

▶ **The background color of your image may clash with the gray background of your Web page. In Chapter 14 you'll learn how to change the background color of both your Web page and of your images. When the background colors of your Web page and your images are identical, you get transparent images, which are all the rage on the World Wide Web.**

2 From the Insert Image Composer Menu, select From File.

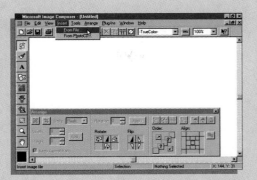

3 Navigate to the folder that has the images you wish to choose from. Photo images are in folders on the FrontPage 97 CD in a folder named\Imgcomp\Mmfiles\ Photos. Clip art is organized in folders found at \Imgcomp\Mmfiles\Web\ Themes on the FrontPage 97 CD.

4 Double-click on a graphic that you want to add to your Web page. The image will be loaded into Image Composer. Click on the image to make it active and then select Copy from the Image Composer Edit menu. The image will now be on the Windows clipboard.

5 In FrontPage Editor, open the Web page that you want to add the image to. Place your cursor where you want to add the image, and press the Enter key to make room for the image.

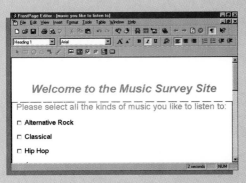

How to Import GIF or JPEG Image Files onto Your Web Page

If you know exactly what GIF or JPEG format image file you want to add to your Web page, you won't need to use Image Composer. You can simply import the file straight into your Web page in FrontPage Editor. You can also import graphics files from the Internet, as long as you know the exact URL of the image file.

On this page you'll see how the image import function works.

▶ ❶ In FrontPage Editor, open the Web page to which you need to add an image.

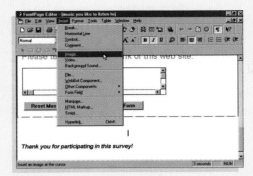

2 Move your cursor to where you want the image to appear. If you want the image centered, click on the Centering button on the toolbar. Then from the Insert menu, select Image.

3 The Insert Image dialog box will appear. The images that are listed are images that are already present in your Web site. You can select one of these images, or you can click on the Other Location tab. Click the From File radio button, and click on the Browse button.

4 The Insert dialog box will open—this is just a typical Windows file open box. Set the Files of Type field to GIF and JPEG. Navigate to the directory where your file is located, highlight the file name, and then click Open.

5 The image you selected will appear on your Web page. Save your Web page and load it into your browser to see how it looks.

How to Edit Graphics Objects

There are a number of properties that can be changed for any image object on your Web page. On this page you'll find out how to access the Image Properties dialog box, and what you can do with the parameters in this dialog box.

▶ **1** In FrontPage Editor, open a Web page that contains an image.

7 You'll learn about using the Default Hyperlink property in the next chapter. When you are finished making changes in the Image Properties dialog box, click OK.

2 Click on the image with your right mouse button and select Image Properties from the pop-up menu.

3 The Image Properties dialog box will appear. In the General tab you will see the file name of this image and the file type. The image will be either GIF or JPEG—you can toggle between the two types. If the GIF image is transparent, the Transparent box will be checked. If the image is interlaced (this means that it downloads fast), the Interlaced box will be checked.

4 JPEG images are compressed images. If you select JPEG, you can specify the Quality, which is a number between 1 and 99. The higher the number, the better quality the image, but the lower the compression rate.

6 In the Appearance tab, you can specify how the image is aligned with the text that is around it, and how much space (in pixels) there should be around the image. You can specify a border thickness (in pixels) if you wish to display a line around the image. You can also specify the size of your image by clicking the Specify Size check box and defining the image size in percent or pixels.

5 In the Alternative Representations section you can specify the file name of a lower resolution picture, and you can specify text to be displayed for anyone who visits your page with a non-graphical browser.

CHAPTER 13

Using Graphics as Hyperlinks

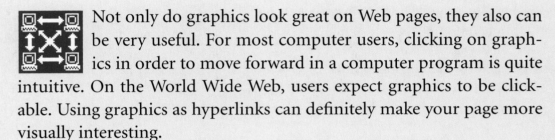 Not only do graphics look great on Web pages, they also can be very useful. For most computer users, clicking on graphics in order to move forward in a computer program is quite intuitive. On the World Wide Web, users expect graphics to be clickable. Using graphics as hyperlinks can definitely make your page more visually interesting.

In this chapter you'll learn how to make a graphic clickable, so that people can click on it to get to a new Web page. And, you'll learn how to create image maps—graphics that contain more than one clickable hotspot.

How to Use Graphics as Hyperlink Objects

In Chapters 9 and 10 you learned how to create text hyperlinks on your Web page. When users click on these hyperlinks they are rewarded with a new Web page, either from the same Web site as the original page or from a new site somewhere out on the World Wide Web. If the hyperlinks were bookmark hyperlinks, then users could click on the hyperlink to move to a different part of the current Web page.

All of this can be done with an image hyperlink just as easily. Instead of highlighting *text* and then clicking on the Create or Edit Hyperlink button to create the hyperlink, on this page you will highlight the *image* and then click on the Create or Edit Hyperlink button. It's that easy.

1 In FrontPage Editor, open a Web page on which you would like to create a graphical hyperlink. If there is no graphic for the hyperlink yet, follow the steps in Chapter 12 on adding images to put a graphic on the page.

7 Save your page and load it into your Web browser to try out your new clickable image!

6 Once you have created the hyperlink, you should check your image properties and make sure that you give your image a border. The border will show up as blue to let visitors know that the image is a hyperlink that they can click on.

2 Select the graphic and click on the Create or Edit Hyperlink button on the toolbar.

3 To create a bookmark hyperlink that will take users to a different part of the current Web page, select the Open Pages tab of the Create Hyperlink dialog box. Click on the down arrow of the Bookmark field to find and select the bookmark you want to hyperlink to. Click OK when you're finished.

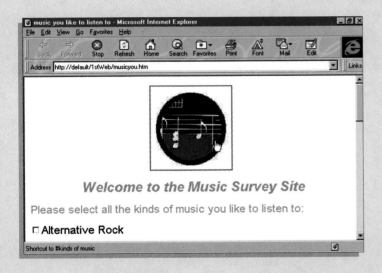

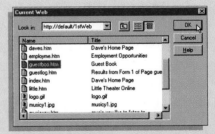

4 To create a hyperlink to a Web page that is part of your current Web site, click on the Current FrontPage Web tab of the Create Hyperlink dialog box. Click on the Browse button to get a listing of the Web pages in the current Web site. Select the Web page you wish to hyperlink to in the Current Web dialog box and then click OK. Then click OK in the Create Hyperlink dialog box.

5 To create a hyperlink to a Web page that is somewhere on the World Wide Web, first find out the page's URL. Then select the World Wide Web tab in the Create Hyperlink dialog box. Make sure the Protocol field is set to "http://," then type the URL into the URL field. Click OK.

How to Create Graphic HotSpots

Image maps are a visually stimulating item that make navigating through a Web site a lot of fun. An image map is a picture on which you define a number of "hotspots." Each hotspot in the image represents a different hyperlink—either to another part of the current page or to a completely different Web page. When users click on the image in a Web browser, what they get will depend on where the pointer is located when they click.

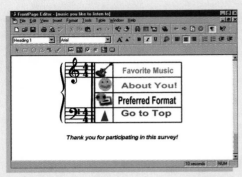

▶ **1** In FrontPage Editor, open the Web page on which you want to make an image map. If the image you want to use is not already on the page, follow the steps in Chapter 12 to add it.

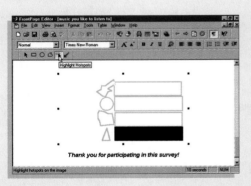

7 If you want to see all of the hotspots on your image map easily, select the image map and then select the Highlight HotSpots button on the toolbar.

2 Select your image. The image buttons will become active on the toolbar. The button with the arrow is the Select button. The three buttons that follow are for defining rectangular, circular, and polygonal hotspots. The fifth button is for highlighting the hotspots, and the last button is for making images transparent—this will be discussed in the next chapter.

3 To create a rectangular hotspot on your image, click on the Rectangular Hotspot button. Go to your image, and click on the top-left corner of the rectangle area you want to define. Drag the mouse to the bottom-left corner and then release the mouse button.

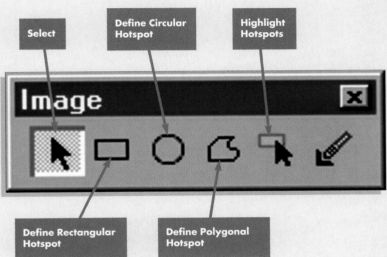

4 The Create Hyperlink dialog box will appear. Follow the steps on the previous page to define your hyperlink.

6 To create a polygonal hotspot, click on the polygonal hotspot button on the toolbar. Place your cursor at one of the corners of the hotspot. Then click on the next closest corner, and then the next, and keep going until you've closed your shape.

5 To create a circular hotspot, click on the Circular Hotspot button. Place your cursor in the center of the hotspot, drag your mouse pointer out to the perimeter of the circle and then release your mouse button.

TRY IT!

The Bartica Little Theater has de-cided that they want to provide visitors to their Web site with a theater graphic and with a Guest Book to sign. They've asked you to create this for them. They would also like you to create a really nice graphical link to the Romeo and Juliet Web page.

Open the Little Theater Homepage that you cre-ated in the last Try It sec-tion.

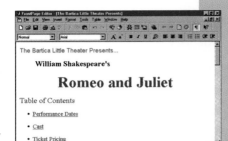

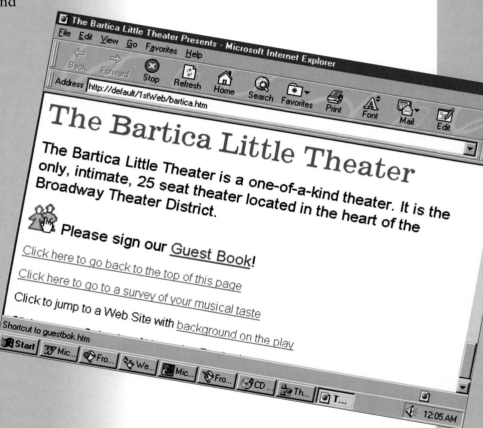

2

Add some introductory textual information about the Bartica Little Theater.

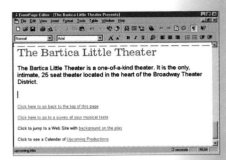

3

Place your cursor at an appropriate spot for an image, and then select Image from the Insert menu.

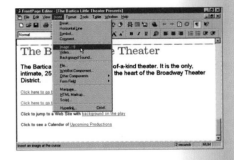

4

In the Insert Image dialog box, click on the Clip Art tab.

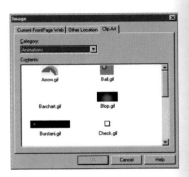

5

From the Category list, select the Icons group and highlight an image. OK the Image dialog box.

6

Right-click on the image in FrontPage Editor and select Image Properties from the pop-up menu.

7

In the Appearance tab of the Image Properties dialog box, size the image to 40 pixels wide, and 40 pixels high, and then click OK.

8

To set up a guest book, type in a sentence indicating that visitors should sign it.

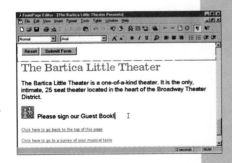

Continue to next page ▶

TRY IT!

Continue below

Now highlight part of that sentence and click the Create or Edit Hyperlink button.

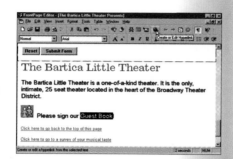

In the Create Hyperlink dialog box, select the New Page tab. Type in a title for the Guest Book and a file name. Make sure that the 'Edit New Page Immediately' option is selected and then click OK.

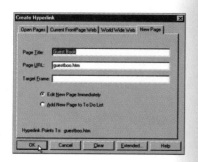

In the New Page dialog box, select Guest Book from the Template list and then click OK.

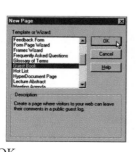

Customize the text, images, and page background in the Guest Book template. Add a background sound.

Replace the author information at the bottom of the template.

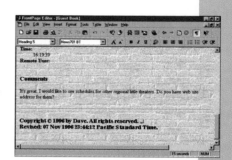

Double-click on the word [Date]. In the Date Bot Properties dialog box, you can edit the format of how the current date will appear on your page. Click OK.

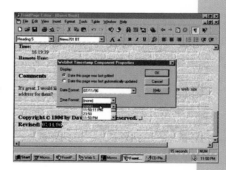

Now save the Guest Book Web page and close it.

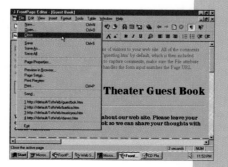

16

Your Guest Book will be linked in to the Little Theater Home Page. Now you can create a graphic for a link to the Guest Book Page.

17

Click on your inserted clip art and click on the Create or Edit Hyperlinks button. We'll use this clip art as a graphic hyperlink to the Guest Book page.

19

Click on the Browse button and double-click the Guest Book Page in the Current Web dialog box. Then OK the dialog box.

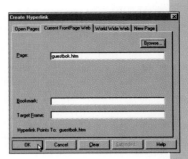

20

In FrontPage Editor, move your cursor over the image and note the hyperlink indicated in the Status Bar.

18

Click on the Current FrontPage Web tab in the Create Hyperlink dialog box.

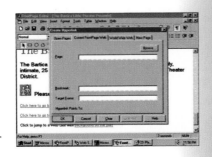

21

Save your Web page and preview it into your browser to try it out!

CHAPTER 14

Modifying the Appearance of Your Page

You may feel that your Web page is lacking something in comparison to other Web pages on the Internet, and you may have noticed that what is lacking is color! The only color you have on your Web pages so far is the color in the graphics you've imported. Your page is gray. Your Web site needs to be decorated, and this chapter is your How-To decorator's guide.

You will learn how to change the background color of your Web page, and how to use an image in the background. You will learn how to make your images transparent.

You will also learn to assign background sounds to your Web page, and explore your options in speeding up the time it takes your page to load in your visitor's browser.

How to Change Your Page Background Color

Changing the background color of your Web page makes an astounding difference to the first impression for Web page visitors. The default gray color isn't bad, but when you visit a Web page that has nice colors you really appreciate the effort. Unfortunately, FrontPage Editor doesn't confine you to only visually appealing colors for your text and background combination. If you want your text to be a glaring red on top of a glaring hot pink background, FrontPage Editor will oblige. So you have to use your own good judgment in choosing a background color, and you have to keep in mind how your text and graphics will look on that background.

▶ **1** Open one of your Web pages in FrontPage Editor.

7 Click OK in the Page Properties dialog box and your Web page will be redecorated with the new color.

6 You can also change default color settings for hyperlinks. However, the default colors are universally recognized and it may confuse your visitors if you tamper with them.

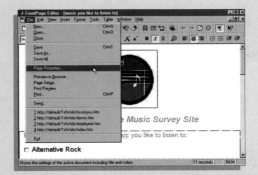

2 From the File menu, select Page Properties.

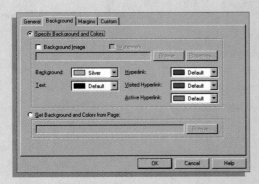

3 The Page Properties dialog box will appear. Click on the Background tab.

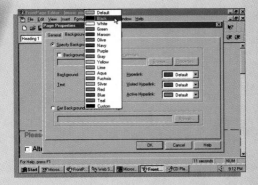

4 From the Background list, select a new background color.

5 You can also change the *default* text color by selecting a color from the Text list. You can still assign colors to selected text, but the Text list in the Background tab of the Page Properties dialog box sets the *default* text color. If, for example, you set your page background to black, your default text color should be white or another very light color.

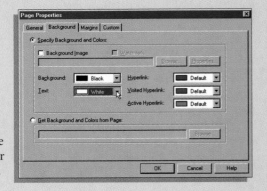

How to Use Background Images

Many of the really professional-looking Web pages that you will come across will have background images. A background image is a picture or pattern that is used instead of a solid background color. When a background image is used, the text and pictures on a Web page sit on top of the image, and the image is repeated so that it covers the entire page.

Using background images can make a page look really great, but you have to make sure you use an image that isn't going to interfere with text and other objects on your Web page.

▶ **1** Open a Web page in FrontPage Editor.

TIP SHEET

▶ **If you try out a background image and you can't read the text on your Web page, then your image is too bright or too busy or both. Try a lighter image that is less complicated.**

▶ **You should use GIF or JPG images for your background. Other images may not be accepted by some browsers.**

▶ **If you choose a large image for your background, you may find that your page looks weird. The top left corner of your page will have the full image, and then you'll have pieces of the image in the right and bottom margins of your page. For this reason, small patterns tend to make better background images.**

8 Click OK in the Page Properties dialog box and your new image will be painted behind your Web page, just like wallpaper.

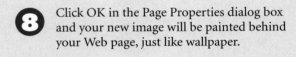
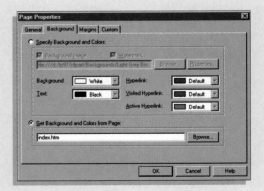

7 You also have the option of linking your page background to another page in your Web. To do so, click the Get Background and Colors from Page radio button and then click on the Browse button and select a page from which to get background and colors.

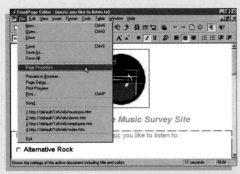

2 From the file menu, select Page Properties.

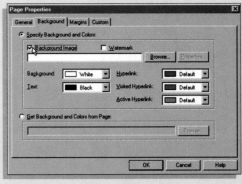

3 Click on the Background tab of the Page Properties dialog box. Select the check box beside the "Background Image" option.

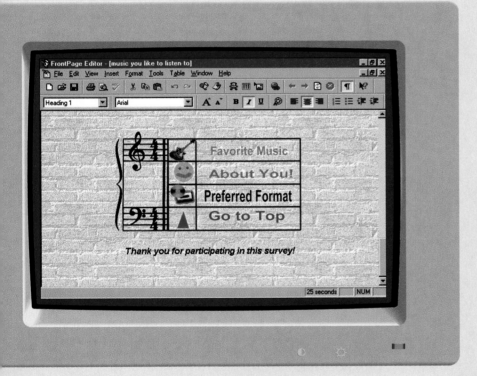

4 Click on the Browse button. The Select Background Image dialog box will appear. Click on the Clip Art tab and choose Backgrounds from the Category list. Scroll through the selection of background images and select an image. OK the Select Background Image dialog box and OK the Page Properties dialog box.

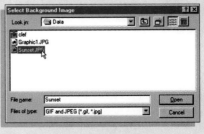

6 Or you can select an image from the World Wide Web by clicking on the From Location radio button in the Other Location tab of the Select BackgroundImage dialog box. You must enter the URL of the picture you want to insert.

5 You could also select an image from your hard disk by clicking on the From File radio button in the Other Location tab of the Select Background Image dialog box. Using the Browse button, you can pick a graphics file from the directories on your hard disk.

How to Assign Background Sounds

The latest versions of Microsoft Internet Explorer and Netscape Navigator can interpret background sound files attached to Web sites. Now there's a feature not every Web page has! You can attach any file in WAV format. Got one of yourself greeting visitors? If not, a cool sound effect or some appropriate music can be an attention grabbing background as visitors browse your Web page.

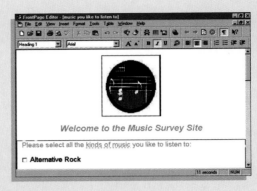

▶ **1** If necessary, open your Web page in FrontPage Editor.

> ► All the fun features we added to our Web site in this chapter increase the time it takes a Web page to load. The "Seconds" indicator in the lower-right corner of your status bar keeps track of the time it will take a browser to load your page if your visitors have a 28.8 speed modem.
>
> ► If your page loading time starts to get longer than 15 or 20 seconds, you might want to reevaluate some of the features you added to your page. Even a small sound file can add five seconds to page loading time. Making GIF images interlaced will help—visitors can see them "fade in" as the page loads.

7 When you're done selecting your background sound and defining how many times you want it to play, OK the Page Properties dialog box, save your Web page, and preview the page in your browser. Sound!

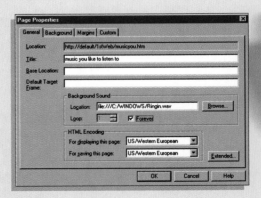

6 You can even elect to have your sound run continuously. For that, click the Forever check box in the General tab of the Page Properties dialog box.

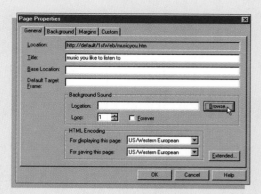

2 Select Page Properties from the File menu.

3 In the Page Properties dialog box, click on the General tab and click the Browse button in the Background Sound area.

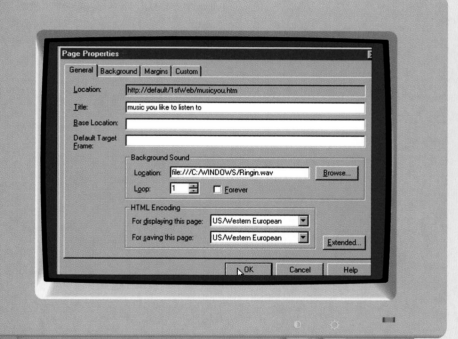

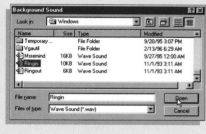

4 Click in the Other Location tab of the Background Sound dialog box if you do not yet have any sound files assigned to your Web site. Click on the From File radio button and click on the Browse button. If you don't have any WAV format sound files available, you should find some sound effects in your Windows directory. Select one and click on the Open button in the Background Sound dialog box.

5 You can elect to loop your sound up to 9999 times, using the Loop spin box in the General tab of the Page Properties dialog box. For some sounds, once is enough!

How to Make Colors Transparent

When you make colors in an image transparent, those colors will not be seen when the image is added to a Web page and that Web page is loaded into a browser. Instead, you will see the background color or image of the page in your Web browser, in place of the color you made transparent. Some image files, including some of the FrontPage clip art, come with white backgrounds. That blends well if your page background is white, but if your background is another color or image, the white background looks odd.

Only graphics files that are in GIF 89a format can have transparent colors. If you attempt to make another type of graphic file transparent, FrontPage Editor will ask you for permission to convert the file to GIF 89a. To see how to make a color transparent, follow the steps on this page.

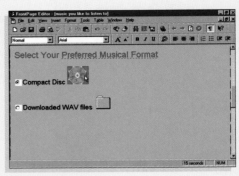

▶ **1** If you don't have a page open, open your Web page in FrontPage editor.

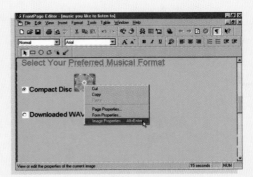

2 Select an image that you want to make transparent. Right-click on it and choose Properties from the pop-up menu.

3 In the Appearance tab of the Image Properties dialog box, set the border thickness to 0 and click OK.

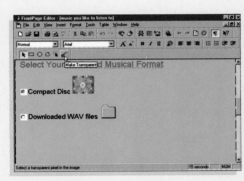

4 Now select the image in FrontPage Editor and then click on the Make Transparent button on the Images toolbar.

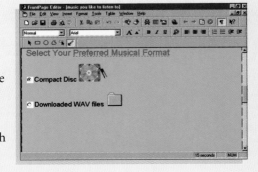

6 Save your Web page. If you change your background color, your image will still be transparent.

5 Your cursor will change into a pencil when it is placed over the image. Click on the color in the image that you wish to make transparent.

CHAPTER 15

Helping Visitors Get Around Your Web Site

The purpose of creating Web sites is to provide information. However, if your Web site is so hard to navigate that visitors can't find the information they are looking for, then you might as well not have a Web site. In this chapter you'll get some hints about making your Web site a nice place to visit, and making your information easy to find.

You already know how to make a Table of Contents using Bookmarks. In this chapter you'll see how to use the FrontPage Table of Contents bot to make one using page headings. And you'll learn how to add a *search bot* to your Web site.

How to Make Your Site Visitor Friendly

The key to making your Web site easy to navigate is consistency. This means that if you have an e-mail link and a home page link at the bottom of some of your Web sites, you should have an e-mail link and a home page link at the bottom of *all* your Web sites. There are a number of ways to make your Web site consistent (without making it look boring). On this page you'll find a collection of hints that will show you how to make use of some of FrontPage's shortcuts to make you Web site really visitor friendly.

▶ **1** Navigational imagemaps are a great way to help visitors get around your Web site. Create a navigational imagemap that contains links to your e-mail address, your home page, your guest book, your table of contents, and any other important page, and then include that imagemap at the bottom of every Web page in your Web site, even the pages that the imagemap links to. After visiting your site for just a few minutes, users will become familiar with your navigational imagemap and will use it to get around your Web site easily.

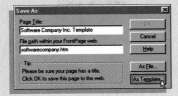

 The best way to create a really consistent Web site is to create a template. If you want every page in your Web site to have a certain graphic at the top of the page, a certain color scheme, and a certain navigational image map at the bottom of the page, then you need to create a template that has these characteristics. To create a template, start with a blank page, and add all of the elements that you want as standard features for all of your Web pages. Then choose Save As from the File menu, and click on the Save As Template button.

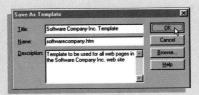

In the Save As Template dialog box, give the template a description, and then click OK. If you've got images as part of your template, you'll be prompted to save them. Now, whenever you need to make a Web page for your site, you choose New from the File menu and choose the template you just created from the template list in the New Page dialog box.

How to Add a Table of Contents

You already know how to make a Table of Contents for your Web page by bookmarking the different sections on your page. But what if you want a Table of Contents for your whole Web site? The Table of Contents bot automatically generates this for you. And if your pages change, the Table of Contents bot can automatically update your Table of Contents.

Just follow the steps on this page to make a great Table of Contents.

1 In FrontPage Editor, open a Web page that you would like to add a Table of Contents to.

TIP SHEET

▶ **The Table of Contents bot works really well when you have a large Web site with lots of well-defined sections and pages. In fact, you can have a whole Web page devoted to a Table of Contents. If your Web site has only two or three pages, you probably don't need to use the Table of Contents bot.**

▶ **If it looks like some of your Web pages are missing from your Table of Contents, check the structure of your Web site by looking at the Outline View in FrontPage Explorer. It could be that you're defining the top Web page for your Table of Contents too low in your Web site hierarchy.**

▶ **If you want to make sure that every page in your Web site is included in your Table of Contents, choose your home page (index.htm) as the top page. This should be the default value.**

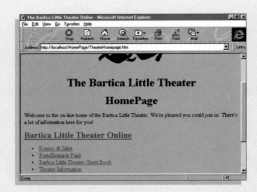

7 Save your Web page and load it into your Web browser. Suddenly your page will have a Table of Contents for your Web site.

2 If there are already a number of headings defined on your Web pages, go on to step 3. If you don't have any defined headings, you should define headings for each of the different sections of the Web page within your Web site. Refer to Chapter 3 for instructions on doing this.

3 Place your cursor where you would like to insert a Table of Contents and then select WebBot Component from the Insert menu.

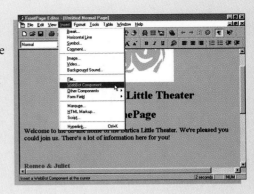

4 In the Insert WebBot Component dialog box, select Table of Contents and click OK.

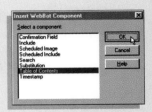

5 The WebBot Table of Contents Component Properties dialog box will appear. Type in the file name of the page that you want the Table of Contents page to generate from. Your Web site is like a tree, and

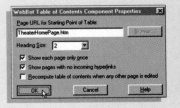

your home page is like the trunk. If you generate your Table of Contents from the home page, then all of the other pages in your Web will be included. If you generate your Table of Contents from some other page, only pages that branch off from that page will be included. In the Heading Size field, choose the lowest heading level that you want included in the Table of Contents. For instance, if you want heading levels 1 and 2, choose 2. Make sure that the "Show each page only once" and the "Show pages with no incoming links" options are selected. These options will ensure that all the pages under the page you selected will be shown, but none will be duplicated. You may want to select the "Recompute Table of Contents" option, but if you have a really large Web site it is not advised. This will be very time consuming and you can get FrontPage Editor to recompute this at any time by opening and saving the Web page on which the Table of Contents is located. When you've made all your selections, click OK.

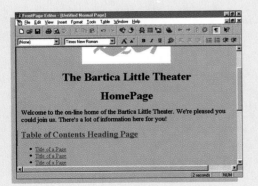

6 In FrontPage Editor you will see a generic Table of Contents. It won't actually list any of the pages or headings.

How to Add a Search Bot

If you've ever visited a Web site to look for some very specific information, you know that the experience can be quite frustrating. You're never sure what specific page in the site will contain the information you need, and if the Web site is huge, you could spend hours hunting for a tiny piece of data. Most big Web sites are now searchable — you can type in a word or phrase and the Web site will be searched for that word or phrase. It used to require some heavy-duty programming to include something like this on a Web page or Web site, but FrontPage Editor's Search Bot makes it easy. On this page you'll learn just how easy it is!

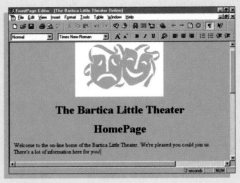

▶ **1** Open the home page for your Web site in FrontPage Editor.

6 The search results will be displayed for your visitors right there on the Web page, and they can click on the page name to go to the page that contains the information they are looking for.

TIP SHEET

▶ **If your Web site is really huge, it's probably a good idea to select the "Score" option in the WebBot Search Component Properties box. This will give all the Web pages that match the search criteria a score, based on how many times the search criteria appears on the Web page or how closely the search criteria was matched.**

▶ **You can put the search bot on a separate Web page, and then you can include a link to it in a navigational imagemap. That way, wherever visitors are in your Web site, they can get to the search page with a simple click.**

2 Type in a sentence indicating that visitors can search for information.

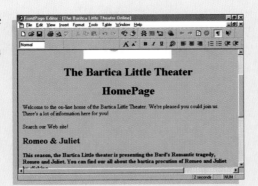

3 Select WebBot Component from the Insert menu. In the Insert Bot dialog box, select Search and then click OK.

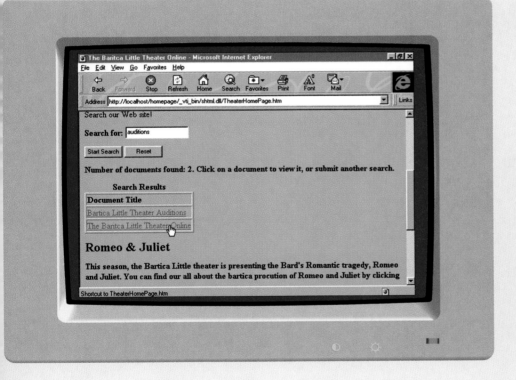

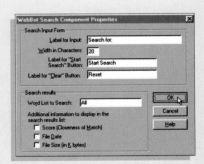

4 The WebBot Search Component Properties dialog box will appear. A search bot uses a form to determine what to search for. You can change how that form looks in the Search Input Form section. In the Search Results section of the dialog box you can specify what the user will see after he or she searches for something. You can leave this whole dialog box with its default values or you can change some of the options. Leave the "Word List to Search" option set to All. Click OK.

5 The search form will show up in FrontPage Editor, but you need to load it into your Web browser to make sure it works.

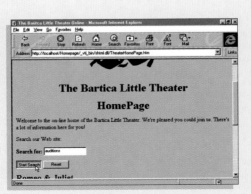

CHAPTER 16

Framing Your Pages

Using frames is like compartmentalizing your Web page. You divide your page up into different frames, and then you can have different URLs appear in each frame. One frame can change URLs while the other frames remain the same, or they can all change at once.

Frames are all the rage on the World Wide Web these days, and most browsers now support frames. Any browsers that don't yet support frames probably soon will. Frames can be very useful. With a framed home page, visitors can check out all of the different pages at your Web site by clicking on a framed table of contents or navigational imagemap. In this chapter you'll learn how to use the Frames Wizard to create your own framed page.

How to Create a Frame Set

The Frames Wizard actually makes it quite easy to create a framed page. It's definitely easier to use the Frames Wizard than it is to define the HTML tags by hand. Frames can get a little complicated though.

It's a good idea to sketch out what you want your frames to look like on paper first. Then you can easily make your choices within the Frames Wizard to get your page to look the way you want it to.

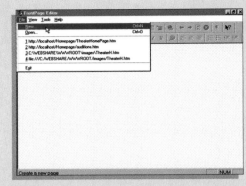

1 In FrontPage Editor, select New from the File menu.

7 FrontPage Editor will not display the framed Web page automatically. This is because you haven't yet defined what will go into each of the frames. That is what you will learn next!

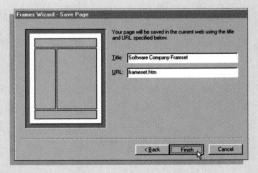

6 Finally, you need to specify a Title and a file name for your frames page. When you are done, click Finish.

TIP SHEET

▶ Once you've become a frames expert, you may decide to design your own frame layout using the Grid option at the beginning of the Frames Wizard. But try out the templates first, until you understand how frames work. Besides, using the frames templates can save you a lot of time.

▶ If you set up a frames page, or choose a frame template and it is not quite what you wanted, don't worry about it. At the end of this chapter you'll see how to edit your frame layout. Most people need to do this once they've got their content on the page. Tweaking the layout is to be expected.

2 In the New Page dialog box, select Frames Wizard from the templates list and then click OK.

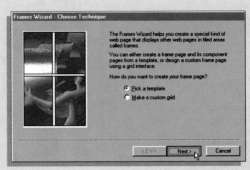

3 The Frames Wizard will first ask you whether you want to use a template for your frames page or whether you want to make a custom grid. Select "Pick a Template" and then click Next.

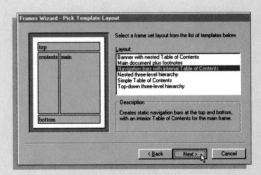

4 In the Pick Template Layout dialog box, you can select any of the listed layouts, and a picture showing the frames layout will appear on the left. Select the layout you want and then click Next.

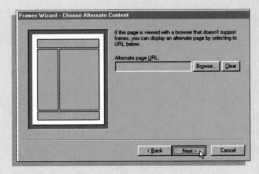

5 The Wizard will now ask if you want to specify an alternate URL for browsers that do not support frames. Specify the URL (or don't bother) and click Next.

How to Frame Web Pages

Now that you've divided your Web page up into frames, you probably want to put something into those frames. You can put pre-existing Web pages into the frames, or you can create new Web pages to put into the frames.

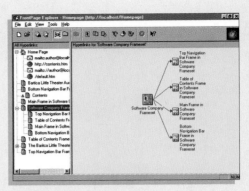

▶ **1** Double-click on your frame page in FrontPage Explorer.

6 When you're all done creating great content with your frame, save your Web pages, and load the frameset page into your browser to see how it looks.

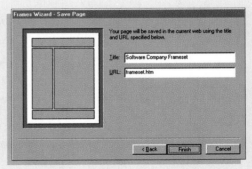

5 When you've finished editing the attributes of one frame, you have to do the same for the other frames in your frameset. Then, click Next and you'll be asked again about the alternate URL. Click Next, and you'll be presented with the file name and title information. Click Finish. You'll be asked if you want to overwrite the file already on your Web, click Yes.

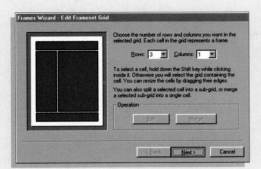

2 The Frames Wizard Edit Frameset Grid dialog box will appear. The frame design you specified earlier will be shown. Click Next.

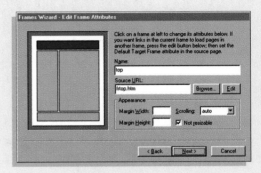

3 The Frames Wizard will now allow you to edit Frame attributes. If you click on one of the frames to the left, you will be presented with all of the attributes of the frame. The Name of the frame is important — later on you can specify this frame as a target for a URL to load into, and you use the Name for this specification. The URL is the Web page that you want loaded into that frame. FrontPage has created a blank page under the filename frtop.htm. You can either use this file name and press the Edit button to edit the Web page in FrontPage Editor, or you can use the Browse button to choose some other Web page to replace frtop.htm. If you click on the Edit button you will be shown a template that tells you the type of information you might want to put in. You have to do one of these in order to get content into your frames page! You can't actually edit the Frameset into FrontPage Editor; you can edit load the individual frames.

4 In the appearance section, you can specify a number of different options for the frame. The margins specify the margins inside the frame — so if you specify 2 pixels of margin both horizontally and vertically, you won't have text running into your frame borders. The Scrolling Field allows you to specify whether scrollbars should never be present, or only be present when necessary. Finally, the "Not resizable" option allows you to specify that users cannot resize that frame in their browser window.

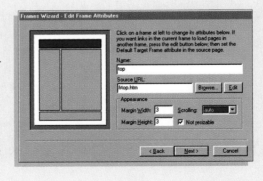

How to Edit Frames

O nce you've loaded your frameset page into your browser, you'll probably think that some of the frames are too small, and some of them are too big, and you'll want to play around with the frame sizes. You can do this in FrontPage Explorer, and on this page you will see how.

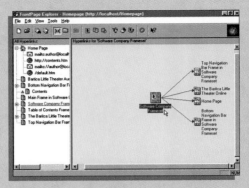

1 In FrontPage Explorer, double-click on the frameset Webpage.

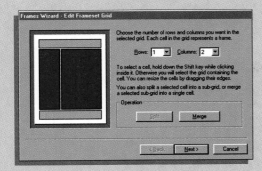

2 The Frames Wizard Edit Frameset Grid will appear. In this dialog box you can select a row or column in your frameset, or you can select a single frame by holding down the shift key and clicking in it.

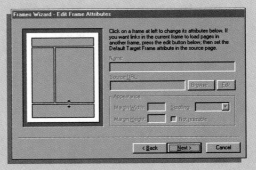

3 You can adjust the frame borders in this dialog box. If you put your cursor right over the border between two frames, your cursor will turn into a double-ended arrow and you can drag the border to where you want it to be. When you're done, click Next. You'll have to go through all the Wizard questions again. If you need to, this is your chance to make other changes to your frameset. If not, just keep clicking Next and then click Finish. You'll be prompted to save over top of the existing frameset—click OK.

4 Save your Web pages and reload your frameset into your browser to see if your changes worked.

TRY IT!

In the past few chapters you've learned how to make your Web page stand out with color and images, and how to make your Web site easy to navigate using frames and other methods. Now that you have this new knowledge, the Bartica Little Theater is anxious for you to put it to use so that you can spruce up their Web site. They want you to make the theater image transparent. They'd like to have a nice background image, and they want their Web site framed.

Open the Bartica Little Theater Online home page that you created.

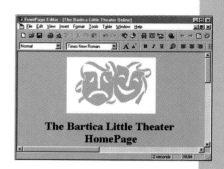

Select the image you inserted at the top of the page. Then click on the transparency button on the toolbar.

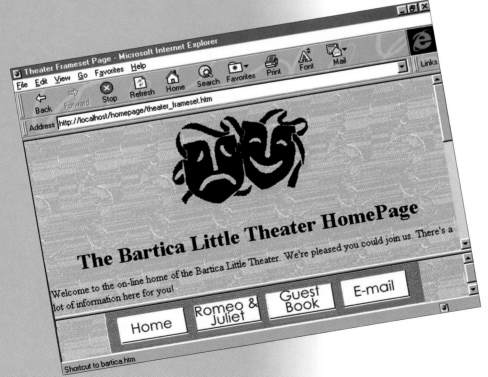

Using the transparency tool, click on the background of your image to make it transparent. If it doesn't become transparent, your image may be too complex. Substitute a less complex image or paint in a more solid background.

Choose Page Properties from the File menu. Select the Background tab and in the Page Properties dialog box, check the Background Image box. Then click on the Browse button.

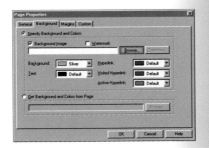

In Select the Back-ground Image dialog box, select an image you want to use for the background of the page. You may have to use the Other Location or Clip Art tabs to get the image from your hard disk. Click Open or OK.

If your background image is dark, then you'll want to make your default text color light. Click on the Text: box button for a color listing.

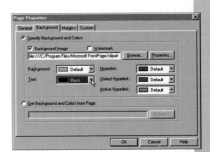

Select a color from the color listing or choose Custom for additional color options.

You may wish to change the colors of your link text as well. When you are finished, click OK to close the Page Properties dialog box.

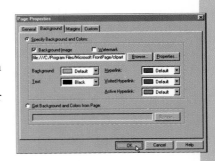

In FrontPage Editor, choose New from the File menu.

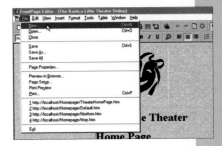

Continue to next page ▶

TRY IT!

Continue
below

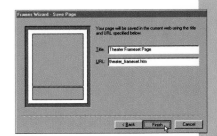

14

Give your
page the title
"Theater
Frameset,"
and a file
name and
then click Finish.

10

In the New Page dialog box, select
Frames Wizard and click OK.

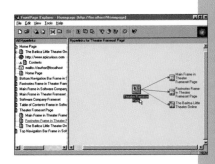

15

Switch to
FrontPage
Explorer and
double-click
on the
Theater
Frameset
page.

11

Select Pick a
Template
from the
Frames
Wizard. Then
click Next.

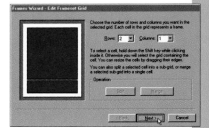

16

In the Edit
Frameset
Grid dialog
box, click
Next.

12

Choose the
Main docu-
ment plus
footnotes lay-
out and then
click Next.

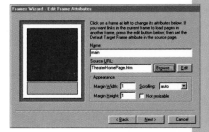

17

In the Edit
Frame
Attributes di-
alog box, se-
lect the top
frame. Then
click on the Browse button beside
Source URL and choose the Bartica
Little Theater home page.

13

Use the
Browse but-
ton to select
the Bartica
Little Theater
home page as
the alternate URL for browsers that
don't support frames. Then click Next.

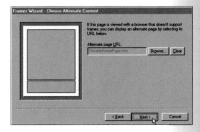

18

Now select the bottom frame and click on the Edit button beside Source URL.

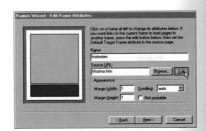

19

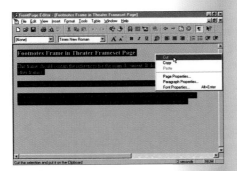

The Footnotes page will show up in FrontPage Editor. You're not going to use it as a Footnotes page, so select the text and delete it.

20

Select Page Properties from the File menu.

21

In the Page Properties dialog box, check the Get background and colors from page: option, and then click Browse.

22

In the Current Web dialog box, choose the Bartica Little Theater Online home page and click OK. Then click OK in the Page Properties dialog box.

23

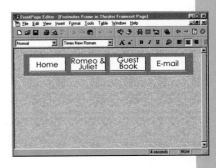

In FrontPage Editor select Image from the Insert menu and insert the image you used as an imagemap. Then define your hotspots.

24

When you define your hotspots, type in Main for the target frame. That way, the pages will be launched in the upper frame.

25

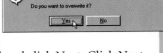

Save your Web pages and then switch back to the Frames Wizard and click Next. Click Next again and then click Finish. You will be asked if you wish to overwrite the page. Click on Yes.

26

You are finished! Load the Frameset page into Netscape to see how it looks!

CHAPTER 17

Organizing Your Web Site with the FrontPage Explorer

 Web sites tend to develop and flourish and grow quite large, especially when you have a tool like Microsoft FrontPage, which makes it so easy to create Web pages. But after awhile, you may find that your Web site is so large that it is difficult to manage and to keep track of all the links and pages. So far this book has focused on FrontPage Editor and has almost ignored FrontPage Explorer. But FrontPage Explorer has a number of very important tools and applications and in the next few chapters you will learn all about them. This chapter in particular shows you how to check the status of the links in your Web site and how to manage these links so that they stay up to date. You'll also learn how easy FrontPage Explorer makes it to import files.

How to Examine Web Site Links

Sometimes, your Web page can contain so many links that it is difficult to remember if you've made a link to a certain page, or what picture files are included in your Web page. FrontPage Explorer has a number of ways of illustrating how pages are linked together in the Web hierarchy. On this page you'll find out what all the little icons in the Hyperlink View actually mean and how to manipulate these icons to change what you see.

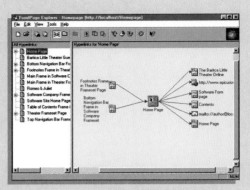

1 Open up your Web site in FrontPage Explorer.

TIP SHEET

▶ As you expand and collapse the different parts of your Web in the Hyperlink View, and as you click on different documents, you'll notice that the Hyperlinks for View on the left shows all the links to and from each page. To see the links to and from a page that isn't in the center of the link view, right-click on the page and from the pop-up menu choose Move to Center.

▶ Image hyperlinks may be toggled on and off by selecting Hyperlinks to Images from the View menu.

▶ You may have noticed that a number of pages seem to be repeatedly present throughout the hierarchy, even after toggling off the Repeated Links view. This is because there are often internal links within a page to bookmarked spots on that page. If you want you can toggle off this option by selecting Links Inside Page from the View menu.

6 There are a number of different icons that represent different types of links. A globe icon represents a link to a page on the World Wide Web. An envelope represents a link to an e-mail address. The portrait icon represents a link to an image and, of course, the house icon represents the home page of the Web site.

5 You may notice that there is another plus sign box within the Theater Frameset Page, and it is for the Bartica Little Theater Online page. You can click on this plus sign as well, and see all the links within that page. In fact you can keep clicking on plus signs until your whole Web site is completely expanded.

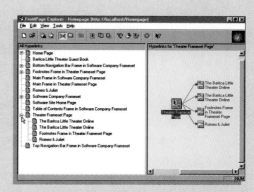

 2 Place your cursor over the border that separates the All Hyperlinks View from the Hyperlinks for View, and drag the border to the right to enlarge the All Hyperlinks View.

3 There are a number of boxes that will appear in the left margin of the All Hyperlinks View. These boxes will have either minus or plus signs in them. If a box has a plus sign in it, you can click on that plus sign (it will toggle to a minus sign) and the document structure to the right of it will be expanded and you will be able to see all of the documents that are linked to and from that page. For example, if you click on the plus sign beside the Theater Frameset Page, you will see all the parts of the Theater Frameset.

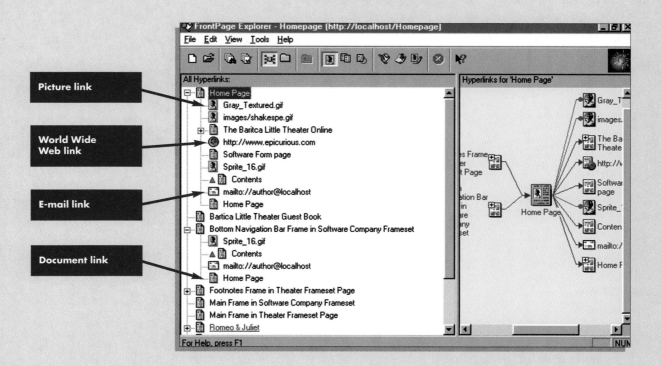

Picture link

World Wide Web link

E-mail link

Document link

4 There are a number of repeated links here. If you don't want to see repeated links, select Repeated Links from the View menu. This will toggle that option off.

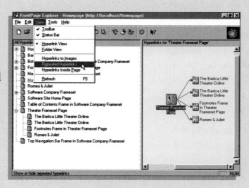

How to Import Files

FrontPage Editor allows you to import files to your Web site. You can import text files, other Web page files, and graphics files. To import a file, follow the steps on this page.

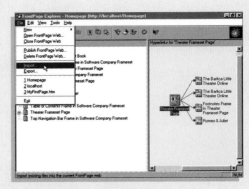

▶ **1** In FrontPage Editor, choose Import from the File menu.

6 The file will not appear in the Hyperlink View of FrontPage Explorer because it has not been linked to any of the pages in your Web yet. However, if you select Folder View from the View menu, you will be able to scroll through and find the file you just imported. It will also be available to you in all Current Web dialog boxes.

TIP SHEET

▶ If you want to add a bunch of files from a certain directory to the Import List, you can select adjacent files by selecting the first file, holding down the Shift key, and then selecting the last file. If the files aren't all adjacent in the directory, you can select them individually by holding down the Ctrl key and clicking on each of them.

▶ The files that you see in the Folder View are listed in alphabetical order.

2 The Import File to FrontPage Web dialog box will appear. There may or may not be some files already listed there. You can add files to this list by clicking on the Add File button, and you can remove files by highlighting them and clicking the Remove button. Click on the Add File button.

3 The Add File to Import List dialog box is a basic Windows file selection box. At the bottom of this box, there is a drop-down menu that allows you to search for files of specific types. Select the type of file you wish to import and then navigate through the directories until you find the file you wish to add to the import list. Select the file name and click Open.

4 The file will now be listed in the Import File to FrontPage Web dialog box. Click OK.

5 The file will be imported into your Web, and its name will disappear from the Import File to FrontPage Web dialog box. Close this dialog box by clicking Close.

How to Verify and Edit Links

On this page you will learn how to run a check on all of your internal and external links to make sure that they are still valid. Of course, performing a link verification doesn't necessarily mean that all of your links still contain valid content, it just ensures that all of your links point to pages that actually exist. If you want to make sure that your links are still appropriate, you'll have to do that yourself by opening the links in your browser.

1 Make sure your Web site is open in FrontPage Explorer.

8 If you don't know what's happened to the link, you may want to take a look at the page on which the link is located. To do this, select Edit Page from the Verify Hyperlink dialog box.

7 In the Edit Link dialog box you can type in the file name or the URL of the Web page that the link is supposed to point to. You can also specify whether you want to update all instances of this link, or only those on certain pages.

2 From the Tools menu, select Verify Hyperlinks.

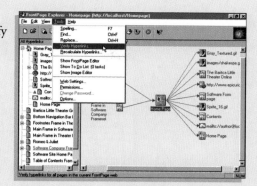

3 The Verify Hyperlinks dialog box will open. All external links in your Web (links to other sites on the World Wide Web) will be listed with a ? status. When you select Verify Links from the Tools menu, all of the internal links are checked, but the external links won't be checked until you click the Verify button. At the bottom of the Verify Links dialog box you will see a message stating how many broken internal and external links you have. Any links that are broken or that have an unknown status are listed inside the dialog box. Unknown links are marked with a ? and broken links are marked Broken.

4 To verify your external links, make sure you are online and then click on the Verify button in the Verify Hyperlinks dialog box. A little globe will appear for the few seconds it takes to verify all the external links.

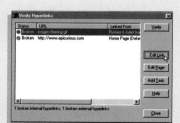

6 You can edit a broken link by highlighting it in the Verify Hyperlink dialog box and clicking the Edit Link button.

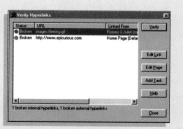

5 When all of the links have been checked, there should be no more with status ?, all links will either be marked Broken or OK.

How to Ensure Continuity of Links

When there are a number of people working on the same Web site, and even on the same Web pages, things can get pretty hectic. And links can be broken because people move pages around or rename them. There are a number of little things you can do that will help make sure that your links stay valid, and that can help you keep track of what's going on within your Web site. On this page you'll learn about the Recalculate tool, which can help you with these types of tasks.

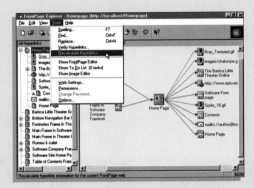

1 If you are running your Web site on your local machine, make sure that you have the Personal Web Server running. If your Web site is on a remote server, make sure that you are online. With your Web open in FrontPage Explorer, select Recalculate Hyperlinks from the Tools menu.

TIP SHEET

▶ When a number of people are working on the same Web site, try to set up a protocol so that files stay relatively organized. Make sure that all images stay in one directory, and try to give images (and any other files) names that will mean something to other people.

▶ In FrontPage Explorer you can right-click on any page and choose Properties from the pop-up menu. The Properties dialog box will give you file information about the page, but it also contains a Summary tab, where you can write in comments or a short description about the page. Filling this in for all of your Web pages can help other people who need to maintain the Web site figure out what pages serve which purpose, without having to load them into FrontPage Editor.

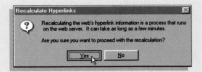

2 You will be prompted to make sure that you actually want to recalculate all of your links.

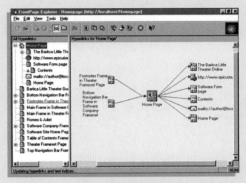

3 Microsoft Explorer will be busy for awhile, and you'll notice the status bar at the bottom will say Updating links and text indices. If your Web site is very large, this updating may take a few minutes. If your site is small it will probably only take a few seconds.

4 When it is finished, the star icon in the upper-right corner of FrontPage Explorer will stop pulsing. But what has really been accomplished? Well, a number of things. If other people are working on the same Web site, you will be able to see any changes, additions, or deletions of pages that they have made—all of the views in FrontPage Explorer will be up-dated. Also, if you have a Search Bot anywhere in your Web site, the list that the Search Bot uses to keep track of the Web site will be updated. All references to pages that no longer exist will be deleted from the Search Bot's list, and all pages that are new will have references added to the Search Bot's list. Thus, all of the links that can exist in your pages should be valid when someone does a search using the Search Bot.

CHAPTER 18

Organizing Files Using Folder View

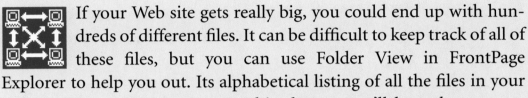 If your Web site gets really big, you could end up with hundreds of different files. It can be difficult to keep track of all of these files, but you can use Folder View in FrontPage Explorer to help you out. Its alphabetical listing of all the files in your Web site is a great resource. In this chapter you'll learn how to use Folder View, and you'll be shown how to upload to your Web site.

How to Examine Files with FrontPage Explorer

In FrontPage Explorer you can switch between Hyperlink View and Folder View with the click of a button. Literally, all you have to do is click the Folder View button or the Hyperlink View button on the toolbar to show each view. You just can't see both views simultaneously. On this page you'll get some hints on using the FrontPage Explorer to look at files.

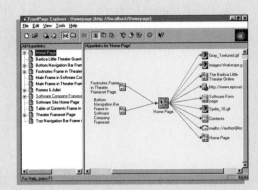

 1 Open your Web site in FrontPage Explorer.

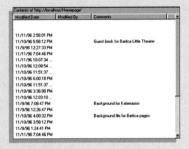

 The sixth column in the Contents is the Modified By column. This lists the userid of the last person to modify the file. The seventh column lists any comments that have been entered into the file's properties information. You can add comments about a file by right-clicking on the Title and choosing Properties from the pop-up menu. The Summary tab in the Properties dialog box contains the text entry area for adding comments about the file.

TIP SHEET

▶ If you just want to load FrontPage Editor, but you don't want it to open any particular document in your Web, select Show FrontPage Editor from the Tools menu in FrontPage Explorer.

▶ If you want to make one of the columns in Contents as wide as that column's widest piece of data, double-click at the border of the column's heading cell.

 Switch from Hyperlink View to Folder View by clicking on the Folder View button on the toolbar.

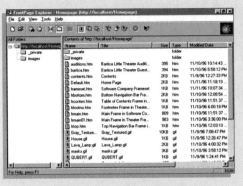

 Folder View offers a lot of information about the files in your Web site. To enlarge the Contents area of the Folder View, drag the border to the left.

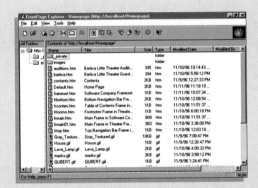

 There are seven different columns of information in Contents. You can use the horizontal scroll bar at the bottom of the view to see all seven. Sometimes, the information for a file is longer than the column width for a certain column. You can widen a column by placing your cursor at the edge of the heading cell, and when your cursor turns into a double arrow, you can drag the column to the left or right to make it wider.

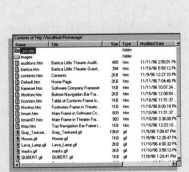

5 The first column in Contents is Name. This column lists the file names for all the files in the Web but without the directory. The next column lists the title that appears in the Title bar when that Web page is loaded into a browser. For other types of files, the Title column contains the file name with the directory. The third column is the size column, and this tells you the size of the file in bytes, in kilobytes (KB), or in megabytes (MB). The fourth column lists the file type. The fifth column lists the last time and date the file was modified.

How to Organize Files and Directories

This section might more aptly be called how files and directories are organized. When you install Microsoft FrontPage, a directory structure is built to hold the various parts of your Web. In this section you will find out what that directory structure looks like and how to find files within it. If you've been wondering where all your Web site files are being stored, this is the page that will answer your questions!

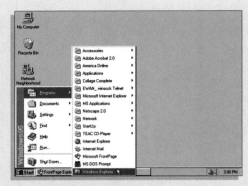

▶ ❶ From your Windows Start menu, launch Windows Explorer.

❺ If you open one of your Web site directories you will see all the system directories, but you will also see a cgi-bin directory and an images directory. If you create any custom CGI scripts (for custom forms), then you would store the script in this directory. When you import image files for your Web pages, they are automatically stored in the images directory for your Web site. Of course, in addition to these directories, you should see all the .htm files of your Web site.

2 You should have a directory right off your root directory called FrontPage Webs. This directory contains two subdirectories: Content and Server. Just like in FrontPage Explorer, you can expand directories by clicking on the plus signs.

3 The Server directory contains three more subdirectories. The contents of these directories are mostly configuration files and executable files that allow you to run the Personal Web Server on your local computer, without a network. However, you should be aware that the Icons subdirectory contains a number of gif icons that you can use on your Web pages. These are icons that the server will use to send messages to Web browsers, but you can import them into your Web site and use them as pictures on your Web pages.

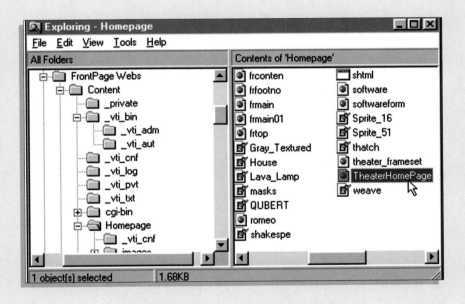

4 If you expand the Content directory, you will find numerous subdirectories. And, if you've been creating localhost Web sites, you will see a directory for each local Web site you have created. In this example there is one local Web site: Homepage. All of the directories that begin with _ are system directories that contain configuration and system files for your Web sites.

How to Upload Your Web Site

Okay, so you've created a Web site on your localhost, you've added lots of pages, and you're happy with it. You've finally found some space on a remote server where you can store your new Web site. The question is, how do you move your entire Web site from your local computer to a remote server? The answer to this question can be found by simply following the steps on this Web page.

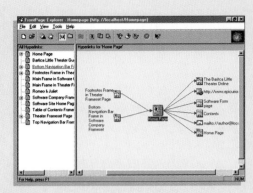

▶ **1** In FrontPage Explorer, open the Web site that you want to upload.

7 The System Administrator in charge of the remote server may have to reboot that server before you will be able to access your remote Web site and test it out. Once this is done you can get access to your new Web site by choosing Open FrontPage Web from the File menu in FrontPage Explorer.

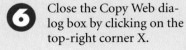

6 Close the Copy Web dialog box by clicking on the top-right corner X.

TIP SHEET

▶ Depending on the server you are uploading to, you may have to include a directory along with the server name when you enter the Destination Server in the Publish FrontPage Web dialog box. Ask the System Administrator of the server you are connecting to.

▶ It's a good idea to warn the System Administrator that you are about to upload your Web. He or she may suggest that you do so at a time when system use is low, because by restarting the system, all other users of the server will have to be kicked off.

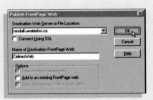

From the File menu, select Publish
FrontPage Web.

The Publish FrontPage Web dialog box will
appear. In the Destination Web Server: field,
type in the name of the server to which you
are uploading your Web site. If you want to
change the name of the Web site, replace the
Web site name in the Destination Web
Name: field. If you want this Web site to become part of a pre-existing Web site on the
remote server select the Add to an existing
Web option. Click OK when you're done.

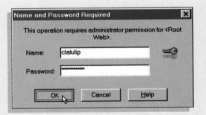

The Name and Password
Required dialog box will
appear. You must type in
the name and password that
allows you to access this remote Web. Then click OK.

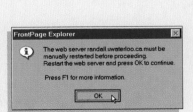

You may then be alerted that the remote Web server must be restarted
before continuing. Click OK.

CHAPTER 19

Configuring Administrator Settings

 If you're not the only one who is going to be creating pages on your Web server, and you want to allow others to create Web sites and log in to the Personal Web Server, then you'll need to define some additional Administrator Passwords. The password you use to create and get access to the FrontPage Server is probably an Administrator Password, unless it's something that's been assigned to you by someone else in charge of your server. In this chapter you'll learn what the different types of passwords are for and how to assign them.

How to Define Administrator Passwords

For any given Web, you can add administrators, authors, and you can define users. Server administrators can perform tasks such as changing the server port number, changing the server type, changing the root directory and uninstalling FrontPage Server Extensions. Authors can create and delete pages. Users are people who will be able to access your Web site from the Internet or your Intranet, using their Web browser. On this page you will find out how to assign Administrator Passwords to people who may need to perform the above mentioned functions.

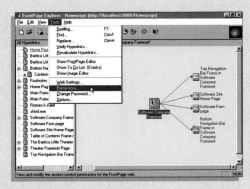

1 Open your Web site in FrontPage Explorer and select Permissions from the Tools menu.

7 When you're done making all the Permission changes, click Apply, and the changes will be made to the Web site's settings. Then click OK to close the Permissions dialog box.

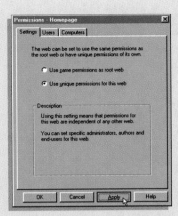

2 The Permissions dialog box will open. If the option Use Unique Permissions for this Web is already selected in the Settings tab, go to step 3. If it isn't, select it and click Apply. You will then have to return to step 1 again.

3 Select the Users tab in the Web Permissions dialog box. To add an administrator user click on the Add button.

4 The Add Users dialog box will appear. Type in a username for the new administrator (usually a first initial followed by the last name). Then type in a password for the new administrator. You will have to type in the password again, to confirm it. Then select Administer, author, and browse this Web in the User Can section. Click OK.

6 You can also specify that the administrators can only perform administrative functions from certain computer systems or networks if you know the IP address or addresses of this system. Simply select the Computer tab and click Add. In the Add Computer dialog box, type in the IP address, using wildcards if there are a number of different IP addresses that the user can log in from. Then select the necessary permissions in the Computer Can section, and click OK.

5 The new administrator's name will appear in the Users list. If you want to remove an administrator, simply highlight the name and click Remove.

How to Add Log-in Passwords

If your Web site contains confidential material that is only meant to be seen by a few select people, you will need to create access log-in usernames and passwords for those people. When you create such things, users who try to load your Web pages will be confronted with a username/password dialog box, and the page will not load unless they enter a valid username and password.

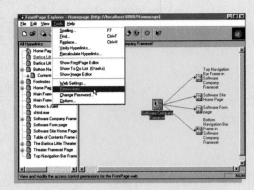

▶ **1** Open your Web site in FrontPage Explorer. From the Tools menu, select Permissions.

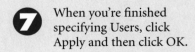 When you're finished specifying Users, click Apply and then click OK.

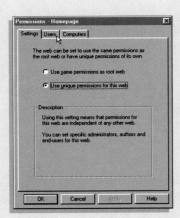

2 In the Permissions dialog box, make sure the Use unique permissions for this Web option is selected. Then click on the Users tab.

3 Select the option Only Registered users have browse access. Then click on the Add button.

4 The Add Users dialog box will appear. Type in the new user's name, and then type in a password. You'll have to retype the password to confirm it. Then select Browse the Web in the User Can section. Click OK.

6 The Add Computer dialog box will appear. You can type in a full IP address to designate a specific machine, or you can type in a partial IP address plus a wildcard (*) to designate that all computers within a certain network should have access. You'll also want to specify permissions in the Computer Can section. Click OK.

5 Alternatively, you can specify that any users logging in from a certain network or machine can access your Web site. Select the Computers tab and click on the Add button.

TRY IT!

Once again, the Bartica Little Theater wishes to make use of your newly learned Web skills. They've heard that you know how to make sure links stay updated, and they want you to check all the Web site links. They've also hired another person to create Web pages for the site (you're just in such demand you can't do everything they need!), so they want you to give the new Web author access privileges to the Bartica Little Theater Web Site.

Open the Bartica Little Theater Web site in FrontPage Explorer.

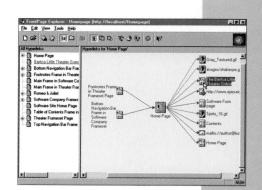

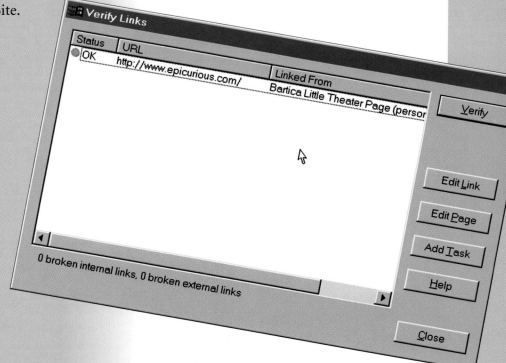

2

From the Tools menu, select Recalculate Hyperlinks.

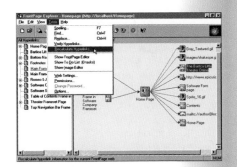

 5

Now select Verify Hyperlinks from the Tools menu.

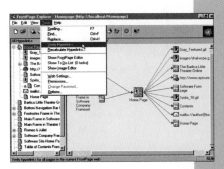

 3

You will be asked if you are sure you wish to recalculate links. Click Yes.

 6

The Verify Hyperlinks dialog box will appear. All the external links from the Web pages will be listed with status ?. If there are any broken links, these will be listed with status Broken. To verify external links, make sure that you are online and then click OK.

 4

The Bartica Little Theater Web Site links will be recalculated and any search 'bots' will be updated.

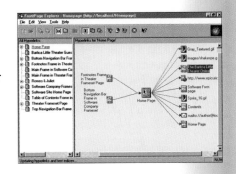

 7

As the links are being verified, the Verify button will turn into a Stop button. If you wish to stop the verification process, click Stop. You will also see a globe and paper icon underneath the Stop button, with an arrow winding around the two objects.

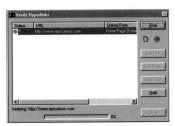

Continue to next page ▶

TRY IT!

Continue
below

10

Make sure
that the op-
tion Use
unique per-
missions for
this Web is
selected.
Select the
Users tab of the Permissions
dialog box.

8

After the
links have
been verified,
they will ei-
ther have a
Broken or an
OK status. If any are broken, use
the Edit URL button to type in
the correct URL, or remove the
links from the Web page.

11

Click on the
Add button
to add the
new author.

9

Now you
must add the
new Web
page author
to the Web
site permis-
sions. Select
Permissions
from the Tools menu in
FrontPage Explorer.

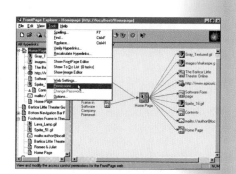

12

The Add
Users dialog
box will ap-
pear. The
new author's
name is Pam Charbonneau, so her
username will be pcharbonneau. Type
this into the Name field. Give her the
word password for the Password field,
and retype this to confirm it. Pam will
be able to change her password to
something private when she logs in and
starts using FrontPage Explorer.

13

In the User Can section of the Permissions dialog box, select Author and Browse this Web.

16

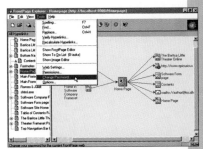

When Pam uses FrontPage Explorer to open the Bartica Little Theater Web site, she will use pcharbonneau and password as her Name and Password the first time. But, she can immediately change her password by choosing Change Password from the Tools menu.

14

Click OK.

17

She will be presented with a Change password for pcharbonneau dialog box. She will have to type in the old password (password) and then she can type in a password of her choice. She must retype this password to confirm it. Then she can click OK and her password will be changed.

15

Finally, click OK to close the Users dialog box.

18

You're all done! The links of the Bartica Little Theater Web site have been recalculated and verified, and the new Web author has been added to the Web permissions listing. Good job!

CHAPTER 20

Maintaining Your Web Site

Once you've uploaded your Web site to a server and people are using it, you'll probably think your job is done. You're wrong—a Web site soon becomes useless unless it is updated constantly. There are very few Web sites where the information that is provided will remain static. The information on most Web pages becomes obsolete after a few days, weeks, or months. It is your job as the Web site author to keep the information up to date. This means changing the data on pages, but it can also mean changing the layout and presentation of your pages if you think they need a fresh, new look. Having a good Web site provider and knowing how to upload single pages can help you with these tasks.

How to Find a Supportive Site Provider

What makes for a supportive site provider? Well, there are a number of characteristics to look for in the company or person who is providing server space to you, and there are a number of features that need to be part of any contract you make when renting server space. On this page you'll learn what these characteristics and features are, and you'll get a few hints on how to find a supportive site provider.

▶ **1** When searching for a Web site provider, you should look for an established company. The Internet service provider business is very competitive but still fairly lucrative because of the growing demand for the service. So there are a lot of new companies popping up constantly. But with the extreme competition, the new companies aren't necessarily surviving for a long time. You want to find a company that has been around and will stay around.

4 To find a good service provider, there are three methods, but only two are preferred. The first method is word of mouth. Ask other Web site authors what company they use for server space, and ask them about cost, throughput, service, and reliability. The second method for locating a supportive site provider is by searching on the Internet. Most large cities have sites that evaluate the local service providers throughput, and some of these listings even show prices and company information. The last method for searching out a good service provider is through the Yellow Pages. Use this as a last resort— it's better to get references from people who've had experience with the company.

TIP SHEET

▶ There seem to be a lot of issues when renting server space. You may be asking, wouldn't I be better off just buying my own equipment? Well, this is a good question. If you have a lot of money to spare, then you may want to buy your own server. But there are a lot of hidden costs in addition to buying the equipment. Unless you're a techno-geek-God you'll probably have to hire someone to be your system administrator. You also still have to pay for your Internet connection, and you have to buy all the software. Unless you plan on going into business yourself to rent out server space to other Web authors, you're looking at an extremely expensive venture!

▶ Keep in mind that if you are planning to rent a large chunk of server space most Web site providers will negotiate a price. Don't just accept the first price they name, they're likely willing to come down a bit if you're going to be bringing them a fair bit of revenue.

2 You should also find out what kind of support services the company offers. If something goes wrong with your Web site, you need to know that there is going to be someone around at the site provider company to help you out. This is especially important if you plan on doing a lot of your Web development during off hours.

3 In terms of your server space rental contract, you should look out for a few things. Make sure that you'll have the ability to rent more space if you happen to run out. This usually isn't a problem, but you should check anyhow. You should make sure that the company has installed the FrontPage Server Extensions. If they have not, don't sign your rental contract until they've agreed to get the latest FrontPage Server Extensions and will continue to update the Extensions as Microsoft releases them. You'll also want to make sure that the company you choose as your site provider has adequate equipment and an Internet connection that provides consistently high throughput.

Updating Selected Files in Your Web Site

To make changes to your uploaded Web site, you have two choices. You can edit the up-loaded version of the Web site by opening it in FrontPage Explorer while you are online. Or, you can edit the local copy and then use a file transfer protocol (FTP) program to copy the single Web page to the remote Web site. The first option is better, but the second option can save you money if it costs you a lot to be online. On this page you'll get a glimpse into both methods.

▶ **①** To edit your remote Web site while online, simply do what you've been doing all along: Open the Web site in FrontPage Explorer (make sure you are online first), and then double-click on the page you wish to edit. When you are done editing, save the Web page as usual and close the Web site. Your changes will be saved to the remote host.

TIP SHEET

▸ **If you choose the first method of directly editing the remote Web site, you have to keep in mind that the local copy of your Web site will no longer be up to date.**

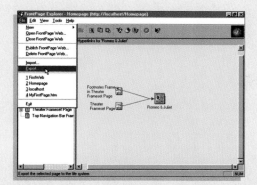

2 If you want to make changes to the local copy of your Web site, use FrontPage Editor to make your changes. Then switch to FrontPage Explorer. In FrontPage Explorer, select the file that you made the changes to and then choose Export from the File menu.

3 The Export Selected As dialog box will appear. This is a basic Windows Save As dialog box. Save the file in .htm format to a temporary directory on your hard drive.

4 You will be notified that the file has been exported to the directory you chose. Click OK.

6 That's all there is to it. Just repeat steps 2–5 for each of the pages you have changed.

5 Use an FTP program to upload the file you exported to the remote server on which your Web site is stored. You will have to find out the exact directory structure of the directories on the host machine to determine where your Web files should go.

CHAPTER 21

Administering
Your Web Site

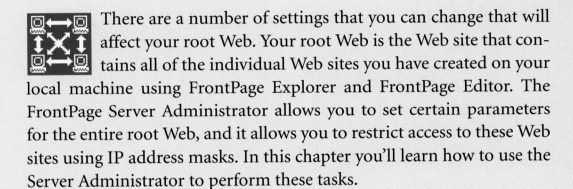 There are a number of settings that you can change that will affect your root Web. Your root Web is the Web site that contains all of the individual Web sites you have created on your local machine using FrontPage Explorer and FrontPage Editor. The FrontPage Server Administrator allows you to set certain parameters for the entire root Web, and it allows you to restrict access to these Web sites using IP address masks. In this chapter you'll learn how to use the Server Administrator to perform these tasks.

How to Reset Configuration Settings with the FrontPage Server Administrator

Using the FrontPage Server Administrator, you can change the Port number for the root Web, you can turn authoring on or off, you can add administrator names and passwords, and you can install or uninstall FrontPage Server Extensions to the FrontPage Personal Web Server. On this page you'll learn how to change the Port number and how to add administrator names and passwords for the root Web.

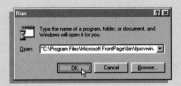

▶ **1** Launch FrontPage Server Administrator from your Windows Start Menu using Run.

6 Finally you can check your Server Administrator settings using the Check button. This check will ensure that everything is set up correctly and that the Port being used is okay.

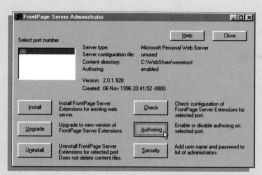

③ You will be asked to confirm that you want to toggle authoring on or off. You can click OK to confirm or click Cancel if you've changed your mind.

② You can toggle authoring on and off by clicking on the Authoring button. When Authoring is turned off, no one will be able to make any changes to the Web sites on the local machine. You won't generally want to use this option, unless you've got your Web site to a perfect state where it will not need any changes again for awhile and you are afraid authors will make changes.

④ If you are running FrontPage on a desktop PC, you will probably only have one Port number listed: 80. However, if you do have other Port numbers listed, you can change the Port number of the root Web by selecting one of the other Port numbers. Keep in mind that 80 is the default Port number, and you shouldn't really change it unless you have a good reason to.

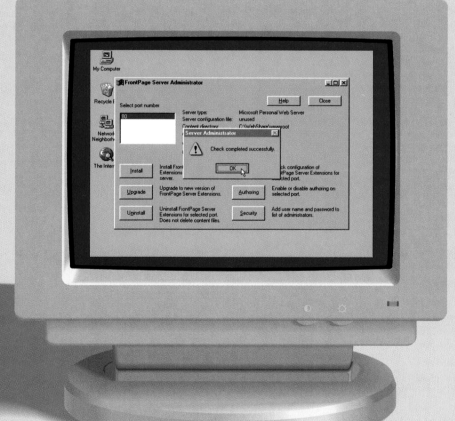

⑤ If you click on the Security button in FrontPage Server Administrator, you will be presented with the Administrator name and password dialog box. You can use this dialog box to add names to the list of administrators for the root Web. Just type in the name of the new administrator and type in a password. Type in the password again to confirm it and then click OK.

How to Restrict Access to Your Web Sites Using the FrontPage Server Administrator

If all of the Web sites within your root Web are confidential and are directed at a specific audience, such as all the employees within a certain company, then you can use FrontPage Server Administrator to restrict access so that only those employees can access those Web sites. All you need to know is the IP address of the network from which all of those employees will be accessing your Web site. If the employees are located in a few separate locations, you can still do this, you just have to find out the IP addresses of each of the locations.

TIP SHEET

▶ Most of the time you won't actually be using a full IP address for your IP address mask. You will often be using part of an IP address and using wildcard (*) characters. For instance the IP mask "133 10 111 *" will allow anyone to log into your Web site, providing that they are logging in from a site with an IP address that has the same first 9 characters and any 3 other characters at the end.

▶ Although it may seem obvious, it is important to realize that if you use an IP mask restriction, your Web site will not be available to the general public who are surfing the Net. You should not use an IP mask just because you want to make sure that a certain network or company has access to your Web site. Only use an IP mask if you want *only* that company or network to be able to access your Web site, and you don't want it available to the public.

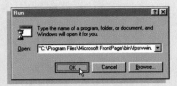

▶ **1** Launch FrontPage Server Administrator from the Windows Start Menu using Run.

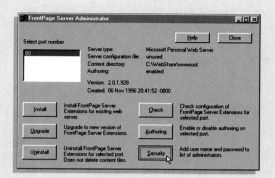

2 Click on the Security button.

3 In the Administrator name and password dialog box, click on the Advanced button.

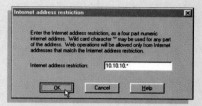

4 The Internet address restriction dialog box will appear. Type in the IP mask that specifies the machine or network that you want to give Web site access to. Then click OK.

5 To add another IP mask to the list of IP addresses that will be allowed to access your Web sites, simply repeat steps 3–4.

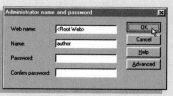

6 When you're done adding IP masks, click OK in the Administrator name and password dialog box.

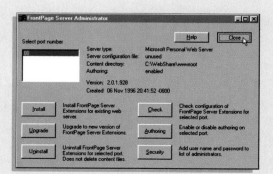

 Finally, click Close to close the FrontPage Server Administrator.

 Choose HTML from the View menu.

3 The HTML for the current Web page will be displayed in the View HTML window. You can see all of the HTML tags that surround each section of text: headings, paragraphs, links for pictures, and so forth. You can edit any of the text in the View HTML window.

4 There are two radio buttons at the bottom of the View HTML window: Original and Current. If you created the Web page from scratch in FrontPage Editor, then the created and original HTML files will be identical. If you imported a file into FrontPage Editor, selecting the Original button will show the original HTML that was imported. Then, if you select the Current button, you will see the HTML that FrontPage Editor has generated for that imported file with the World Wide Web tab on top. Enter the changed URL in the URL field. Then click OK.

How to Edit HTML Code

You can edit the HTML code in the View HTML window in FrontPage Editor. You can edit the HTML code that FrontPage Editor generates. On this page you'll see how to do this.

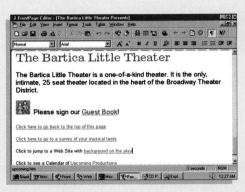

▶ **1** Open your Web page in FrontPage Editor.

5 When you have finished editing FrontPage's generated HTML code in the View or Edit HTML window, click on the OK button. Changes made to your HTML code are saved as part of the FrontPage file, and are reflected when you view the file in the FrontPage Editor.

TIP SHEET

▶ **If you are quite familiar with HTML tags, you can use the Extended button in any FrontPage Editor dialog box to add extra tags that FrontPage Editor is not familiar with. For example, if you want to add extra tags to an image that specifies something, you simply right-click on the image, choose Properties from the pop-up menu, and then click on the Extended button in the Image Properties dialog box. In the Extended Attributes dialog box you can add extra tags that FrontPage Editor cannot directly implement.**

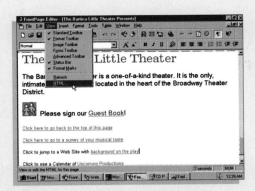

 Select HTML from the View menu.

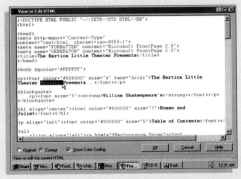

3 You can edit text in the View or Edit HTML window.

4 If you have studied HTML coding, you can make changes to the HTML code directly in the View or Edit HTML window. The View or Edit HTML window is a text editing program that lets you cut and paste, insert, and delete text.

How to Find HTML Resources

This Appendix has demonstrated how to edit the HTML code behind the Web pages you create in FrontPage Editor, but it really hasn't demonstrated what HTML tags are for and what you can do with them. That is a subject which would take another book entirely. Therefore, this section offers you information on where to go to find out about all the HTML tags, what they are used for, and how to manipulate them.

▶ ❶ First of all, there is another book in this "How to Use" series, called *How to Use HTML 3.0*. The book is by Scott Arpajian, a veritable HTML God — he creates Web pages for the ZDNet World Wide Web Site. You can purchase this book at local book stores. It will explain, in easy-to-follow steps, everything you need to know about HTML 3.0, which is the most recent international standardization of HTML.

2 The Internet is, of course, another great resource for information about HTML. The following Web sites, which were mentioned in Chapter 1, are great resources for HTML information:
- A Beginner's Guide to HTML:
  http://www.ncsa.uiuc.edu/General/Internet/WWW/HTMLPrimer.html
- A Guide to HTML Commands:
  http://www.woodhill.co.uk/html/html.htm

3 A few additional links that might be useful:
- The Netscape extensions to HTML 3.0 page:
  http://home.netscape.com/assist/net_sites/html_extensions_3.html
- A page of Selected HTML 3.0 Examples:
  http://www.ozemail.com.au/~dkgsoft/html3/index.html
- The Netscape Frames reference page:
  http://home.mcom.com/assist/net_sites/frames.html
- The Microsoft Internet Explorer How-to Guide:
  http://www.microsoft.com/ie/most/howto/

INDEX